FROM BEING A MAFIA WIDOW TO GOD'S CHILD

I will be a Father to you, and you shall be My sons and daughters, says the Lord Almighty.

By

Robin Colombo

FROM BEING A MAFIA WIDOW TO GOD'S CHILD

Copyright © 2020 by Robin Colombo

DEDICATION

To God the Father and Jesus Christ for never giving up on me. I would still be lost in darkness without them.

To my beautiful children, Jennifer Nicole Ethridge, Frankie Gennaro Colombo, my grandson, Tyler Bryce Simmons, Kevin Simmons, Lilac Colombo and Madison Clark

To my dad and mom for putting up with all my transgressions over the years.

To the Colombo family, for all we've endured, we're still family. To the memory of my late and only husband, Gennaro Colombo.

Also, to my first love, Curtis Ethridge.

I love you all with all my heart and soul. May God bless you.

I know that You can do everything. Job 42:2

TABLE OF CONTENTS

CHAPTER 1

THE CHILD AND THE LAMB

It seems I've always been in a hurry, even to be born. Instead of nine months, I felt compelled to present myself early, at eight months. I was raring to get going in this old world, yet I just didn't know what trouble the world had to offer.

I was born in Charleston, South Carolina, on September 21st, 1961, the youngest of three siblings. Being the baby, my older brother and sister—not wanting to be bothered by their younger sister—kind of left me alone to my own devices. No problem. Their near avoidance of me allowed me to be blessed with a carefree, independent spirit. At least I thought I was blessed. I was soon to find out at an early age that my carefree spirit was not such a blessing after all.

My father was a military man, which meant our family moved around every couple of years. I had to be ready to meet new friends, even though I never really developed any relationships or true friendships at all. With the military moves of my father, I met some very nice people, but my friendships were short-lived.

When I was four, we moved to Greece for my father's assignment. In Greece, there were not a whole lot of neighborhoods like we have in the United States, so meeting kids my age was very difficult, if not impossible. My best friend was my dog, Frisky, a gorgeous purebred

German Shepherd. He was big and regal looking, like the kind you would see modeling for a famous brand of dog food. He and I would go from door to door and introduce ourselves. Knowing only the basic introductions in Greek, and my neighbors knowing no English at all, we just stood at the doorstep looking at each other. They usually smiled, patted my head, and invited Frisky and me into their homes. I remember sitting at their big wooden tables, feet dangling and looking intently as they talked and cooked. I was fascinated at all the pasta they made, and after a while, they would load me up with their delicacies and I would be on my way home.

Back in the 1960s, in Greece, parents just didn't worry about some stranger picking their child up and harming them. This was a good thing, because I never met a stranger. However, I was warned about the gypsies, the kind you read about in books.

They looked like American Indians who wore a bunch of long beaded necklaces, having their arms covered in bangles and bracelets and wearing different colored baggy clothes. Many of the women looked like Madam Ruby, your proverbial fortune teller at the county fair. We were told not to have anything to do with them, as they liked to kidnap little blonde kids. With my dark hair, I felt safe.

One day, while playing with Frisky, I noticed some gypsies coming up the road. Even though there was a language barrier, I knew they wanted to trade what they made by hand for anything we had of value. I ran into the house to grab my father's favorite Beatles album and some of my parents' other belongings. With my free spirit, I just loved trading what wasn't mine for free stuff from the gypsies. Right in the middle of my big deal, however, my mother came out and caught me. My mother's fear of the gypsies led to her pouring her anger upon me. She chased them off and scolded me.

I argued with my mother, saying that Frisky would take care of me by growling and barking at anyone that he thought would harm me. This even transferred over to my older siblings, so much so that my mother was afraid my precious doggy pal would bite one of them. The fear of a mother for her children prompted her to get rid of Frisky. This was the first time I lost anything dear to me. Oh, I was brokenhearted. The wounds of a little heart left unattended would give future hurt such an easy entrance.

One day, on my little jaunts around the neighborhood, I saw a hole under the fence, just big enough for me to crawl under. With Frisky gone, I found a new friend to play with every day. It was a baby lamb. I didn't have to worry about my little black lamb hurting anyone, and even though he wasn't mine, I still considered him my baby. We would roll around in the grass, and I can remember how I giggled as he licked my face or nudged me. Many times, I tried to carry him, but to no avail. I wanted to carry him like a baby. My lamb more than made up for the loss of serious-looking Frisky. My little lamb was innocent and playful.

One afternoon, I was sitting alone on my front porch while my brother and sister were riding their bikes. They rode by and yelled, "Ha, Ha! Robin's lamb is being killed!" I jumped up in a state of panic and ran to where my lamb lived, hoping they were lying.

I crawled through the hole in the fence and ran to where grown-ups were standing around a man on a ladder. I broke through the crowd and looked up to see my baby lamb hanging from a tree being slaughtered. I screamed, "No!! He's mine, please stop." The crowd sent me away. I was crying my heart out when my mother met me in the middle of the road. My mother tried to comfort me by taking me to the square for a walk. This seemed to help me some, as people would come up and call me by name and ask how I was doing. Still, at the age of four, the loss of my lamb added to the loss of Frisky.

With so many loving me the way they did, I really did not know any strangers. They were all my friends. I thought I had gotten over the loss of my baby lamb. Little did I know that the stain left in my heart would affect me all through life.

The next year, at the age of six, with everyone supposedly my friend, an older Greek man forced me into his house, threw me on his bed, and proceeded to have his way with me. Being the spitfire that I was, I started screaming, fighting, and then biting him. I got away, ran out the door, and to my home, where I was safe. This incident left me with great fear and distrust that would affect a big part of my life.

These three early events in my life robbed me of much of my childhood. I had an early knowledge of the evil and pain this world had to offer. At age five, there was really no more child and no more lamb— not until later, that is. A child and a lamb were to be resurrected in my life, as you will see.

CHAPTER 2

REBELLION

We lived in Europe for several more years, until I was eight, when the military moved my father back home to the United States.

At the age of eight, while attending a slumber party, I was introduced to the Ouija board. I began to play with it and began having innocent seances. Unfortunately, these innocent seances would open up doors for evil to enter into my playground. Shortly after I began to play this game, I also began seeing transparent figures on the ceiling, which I later became aware of as demons. Through this door to darkness, I would later try to find comfort and communicate with lost loved ones.

Moving into rebellion in my early teens, I so desired to be out on my own. I left home several times, only to be brought back. My father tried to beat the rebellion out of me with a belt. Being the military man that he was and being the type of man who brought that long-term, ingrained training with him everywhere that he went, he also, of course, brought it home to us. I do not necessarily feel that he was doing something "wrong" – it was just a way of life for so many families back then, during that time. In our house, as in many other houses, you played by the rules or you were punished for not playing by them with a physical reminder of why you should. For me, of course, these incidents stemmed from my rebellious nature and my insistence on carrying out almost every idea that crossed my mind, even if it was unhealthy or unwise.

Please keep in mind that this was the sixties and the seventies: homes were run quite differently back then from how they are right now. Back in those days, parents did not go into therapy to learn how to parent in the way that they do now. Family therapy was not a common practice, if it was a practice at all. As for me, I had rebelled since I was three years old, and bucking against the status quo of life, my family, and society's rules was just something that I did. I was a rebel through and through. Sometimes, I thought that the rebellion was in my blood, so rooted was it in my sense of self and how I appeared and behaved with others around me.

What my father was actually doing was beating more scars and wounds into an already damaged spiritual heart. It seems by fifteen, I was on my way to self-destruction, wanting to be free and go my own way. I didn't care much for education, always thinking I would meet Prince Charming and we would live happily ever after.

As I rebelled against all authority, I was really not under any authority. Therefore, I had no real boundaries and was open to every vain thought or feeling that came along. Now, of course, I understand that all of these behaviors seemed like such a deeply ingrained part of me for a reason: I have since been diagnosed with Bipolar I disorder. However, at the time that I was coloring my teenage years with the shades of fighting back against any and all authority, I didn't know that. Any time that something did not go my way, I would simply run the other direction, even if that direction led me straight into an unhealthy behavior, habit, or relationship. But I didn't know any better, so I stayed on my path of destruction for far longer than I might have if I had known then what I know now, and if the resources that are available to others in situations that are similar to mine had been available to me at any point in time.

I moved out from my parents' home at age seventeen. I never experienced much love from them. My mother never told me she loved me. I found out much later on that her mother never told her she loved her, either.

Thanks to how I had been raised, and the struggles that my family and I had gone through to try and understand each other, to all live under the same roof, I had often felt unloved. My father's military style left something to be desired in our relationship. It often seemed so cold to me; I felt unloved by him as well as by my mother. I didn't understand his background and the rules that he lived by since I was just a child, and so moving out a little younger than many people are when they leave home for the first time seemed like a natural next step for me. I suppose that when I look back now, I was rebelling even at becoming an adult.

One night at a party, I thought I had met the love of my life in Curtis Ethridge. He was tall, dark-haired, and handsome. They say women choose mates that are like their fathers. Not so with me, as my father and Curtis seemed to be opposites. Curtis played lead guitar in a band while selling drugs on the side. I thought he was cool, tough, and very popular. All the women adored him.

His father owned his own company and had been a racecar driver in the past. Curtis had even won a few races himself. He was very adventurous. My kind of man!

Curtis's parents were divorced, yet I thought and still think his mother was some kind of saint. Back in the 70s, she would have been called a Jesus freak. She was a lovely woman and always very, very nice. Yet, with my rebellious heart, I saw her as very uncool.

Several months after Curtis and I started living together, I found out I was pregnant. We discussed getting married, but at a later date. I was set on having this baby, but Curtis talked me out of it. Abortion was just another form of birth control for me, and I never once thought of it as murder. Before or after the abortion, I never even thought about going to God. He was a stranger to me, but as I was to find out later, He knew me for all of time. It did not matter to me that Curtis's mother had a direct line to God. I needed to have my own, but that wasn't for some time to come.

My relationship with Curtis mainly consisted of rock 'n' roll, drugs, and drinking, plus, being with the in-crowd—or so we thought. We were very jealous of each other, two people living together, yet living for ourselves exclusively. Living this very selfish life, we came to hate each other because of our own self-hate, and we didn't even know it. Our hate turned into physical and verbal abuse. Curtis, being physically stronger, had a much deeper anger than I had. As a result, he beat me more and more. One time, he nearly broke my eardrum. Curtis almost completely controlled my life, never allowing me to work. Yet, we maintained some kind of sick love relationship. My first love, my Prince Charming, turned into a man who harmed me and tore my heart apart. There came a breaking point in me that made me leave him when I was pregnant.

In 1981, at age twenty, I had a beautiful daughter, Jennifer Nicole Ethridge, conceived out of wedlock. Curtis and I never did tie the knot. There was nothing good about our relationship—nothing— except our beautiful daughter. She was the most beautiful baby I had ever seen. I would be with Curtis on and off for several years, while staying with my parents and working intermittently.

After I finally left Curtis, my focus turned to little Jennifer. In the back of my mind, I was always thinking I could raise her and give her everything she could want. At least I was a little less selfish now, but was mistaken about what true love for Jennifer would be—giving her things! At a pretty young age, my heart was broken. Then, through my own self-seeking lifestyle, my heart hardened, so I couldn't receive or release any true love. It was sad that I didn't know how to really love my own daughter. I thought that inanimate things could satisfy the soul of this precious little girl. My life was definitely on the road to destruction with no construction in sight!

LOOKING FOR LOVE

was working as a secretary at a real estate office when Jennifer was born. I became close friends with one of the realtors, Trish. I was helping her out after her divorce, and I took her to apply for a bartending job. She told me I should apply to be a cocktail waitress. I did, and I made more money in one night than in a whole week as a secretary—and it was a whole lot more fun.

My parents kept Jennifer on the weekends, giving me time to work and play at the bar. I found I could make more money in almost one night than I could working a full week as a secretary! So long, office job! Money became the most important thing to me, because it bought my freedom from having to depend on a man ever again. It's amazing what the human mind and heart can conceive as freedom.

While working in the bar business, some of the members of the famous southern rock group Lynyrd Skynyrd came in as customers. Most of them lived in the Jacksonville area. The first time I met them, they called me over to them. They invited me and Trish to breakfast, and Leon Wilkeson, the bass player, invited us to his home to watch movies with a few members of the band. We smoked pot, we drank, we laughed, and we had fun. We exchanged phone numbers, and we stayed in touch and became really close.

One night, I took them home to meet my parents, but my father wasn't enthused or impressed. However, for someone in their 20s or 30s, the group was awesome. Trish and I tried to keep a nonchalant composure when we walked into nightclubs with Lynyrd Skynyrd. The lights would shine on us, and our entrance would be announced. I felt like a movie star.

I had a romantic fling with Alan Collins, the lead guitar player for Lynyrd Skynyrd. I met him separately from the rest of the group. I met Alan through my daughter's uncle, who was a friend of his. Alan was a very funny man; we were constantly laughing together. He often made fun of my cooking skills, because I didn't have any. I teased him about the fact that I could hardly get him to wear shoes when we left the house. He could dress up, but he hated to put on shoes. Alan had a black Mercedes that was $80,000 in the 80s, and he would let me drive, but I wouldn't go fast enough for him, so he would take back over driving. He gave me gifts, like plants and flowers. He asked me if I needed anything for my apartment, but my pride wouldn't allow me to accept. He wanted to take me out of town, but I had obligations with work, and I didn't want him taking care of me.

There was no real love connection—I only liked him for what he did. Neither his fame nor money could grip my heart, because of my old heart wounds from Jennifer's father, Curtis. I was searching for happiness and true love, but had no idea how to fill the emptiness I was feeling.

At twenty-three, I met a man named Doug who was thirteen years older than me. He was small and dark and reminded me of Sonny Bono. He was very wealthy, and we ended up living together for four years in a 4,000 square foot home on St. John's River in Jacksonville,

Florida. Doug was a very stable guy, a non-drinker and non-smoker, and was able to give a girl all the security one would want. But I was not able to follow through with marrying him. During those four years of living with Doug, I kept busy managing a bar and restaurant, O'Malley's, making it a very successful place, personally handing out cards and inviting people to a friendly atmosphere. I loved my job. It gave me so-called independence from Doug, even though he was a nice guy. I started drinking every night, and if I had stayed longer than the five years there, I know I would not be living today.

Doug was ready for marriage, settling down, and having a real, committed relationship. All that I thought I was looking for—real love—I couldn't receive or release. It just wasn't in me to do. None of the jewelry, clothes, sports cars, and nice homes Doug had to offer would persuade me to give myself to anyone completely. I realized it was more a matter of *couldn't*, rather than *wouldn't*. I just could not give my love or life to anyone.

After leaving Doug, I reverted to my old habits of drinking and partying through managing a club. I sure wasn't managing my drinking. I brought this club from its grand opening to a very prosperous business. I loved people, being very outgoing, and I was used to passing out cards about the club at businesses and to virtually anyone I thought wanted a fun-loving time. After five years of doing this, my brain was becoming clouded with alcohol and drugs.

I was looking for some adventure in my life. I began to move around a lot and got involved in stealing clothes. This seemed like such a rush that I really didn't care about the consequences.

I had been shoplifting for quite some time by the time that I was officially caught for it. I had done it so often that I don't really even know or remember the particular circumstances under which I was busted. I shoplifted often; the rush of adrenaline and the thrill of feeling as though I was truly alive were too good to let go of or pass up. The first time that I had stolen something, I was only twelve years old. I don't know why I did it, or where I had gotten the idea from at such a young age. I didn't try to steal anything big – just a pencil and an eraser. In the middle of it, my mother caught me taking it and demanded that I put the little pencil and eraser back right away. I did.

Later, I stole something much bigger – a whole entire outfit. I got away with it that time: no one caught me in the act, no one made me put everything back on the shelves and hang them back up on the racks. I walked out of that store feeling like I was flying from the high of not only the rush of knowing I was getting away with it, but also the rush of the act, itself. That thrill kept me coming back for more again and again and again. I stole so many times in my life that I honestly don't really recall the difference between the things that I purchased above board and the things that I owned that I had taken without paying.

I would go in waves with my shoplifting. I would steal anything and everything that I could get my hands on for months on end, and then stop, out of the blue, for no reason at all. I'd go for a little while without lifting anything and, then, the need for the rush would overtake me and I'd go straight back into it. I would have the money on me to be able to buy something, and I would steal anyway. I usually stole clothes or makeup, although those weren't the only things.

It wouldn't be until I was in my thirties that I would start to see a therapist who pointed out that these thrill-seeking aspects of my nature were due to my bipolar disorder. Stealing, risky behavior, partying, drinking, doing drugs, having volatile relationships – these were all a part of my disorder. Now there's a list of all of these behaviors for anyone to check out, but at the time, I was basically just a guinea pig. I was told that I had a "chemical imbalance". At the time, though, I was just self-destructive, and the stealing was a big part of that. Every time that I did it, I knew that I could be caught at any moment. When I was finally caught, however, it was a lot worse than I expected. I ended up being sentenced to two-and-a-half years in jail, but due to my clean record – no real crimes in my past – I served a total of six months behind bars.

In 1993, in Dayton, Florida, I was caught for shoplifting—a grand theft charge. Instead of sending me to prison, the judge sent me to a rehabilitation facility. The rehab facility where I ended up living was nothing like most of the rehab places you see on the news and read about in the magazines today. It was not particularly glitzy, it definitely did not take itself at all seriously, and to be completely honest, it was kind of a joke. Nowadays, rehab places are usually very strict and regulated. Where you go, when you wake up, what you eat, and the doctors that you see are all very serious about getting you through your addictions or your difficulties.

For me, though, rehab wasn't even really a punishment. It was very lax there; there was almost no structure to speak of. In fact, since I was there, it has been closed down, probably because it was not a particularly good place to rehabilitate people from their crippling addictions. The days were never very regimented: you would wake up, have breakfast, make up your own bed, and then head to group therapy. Group therapy primarily consisted of all of us who were staying there sitting around in a circle and talking about things – mostly drugs, using drugs, what our lives were like while we were using drugs. It wasn't anything like it is now, where most of the time you're receiving both individual and group therapies that attempt to get to the bottom of why you're really there in the first place.

My rehab facility was in the projects, and it was essentially an apartment building. Every person who was in there had their own apartment, and we all really did our own thing when group therapy was done. No one really had – or expected – any accountability, from the staff or from the residents. Of course, at the time that I was in there, I certainly didn't take it seriously at all. I did not think that I was a drug addict, and so the therapy – or what passed for therapy – didn't have much of an effect on me. I don't know if it helped anyone else. I was casual friends with most of the people in there because my nature is to get along with almost everyone, but I couldn't recall now any of their names or any conversations that we may have had.

At this time, I was having a relationship with a retired federal agent who lived in another city. He would give me money, a stereo, a television, clothes, jewelry, and anything else I needed. But, just like all the other men in my life, the things they had to offer just didn't fulfill my desires.

While I was living at the rehab facility, I worked in an optical shop in the mall in Daytona. One day, I went in to see the doctor about something, and he informed me he had a Colombo in his office, and for me to wait. I waited patiently. Then, two men walked out of the office.

The definitely Italian client, Jerry Colombo, said hello to me, and we made eye contact with each other. I took care of the matter I originally came in for, and went back to my office.

Later, I found out that after I walked away from the doctor's office, Jerry said to his Uncle Tommy emphatically, "I'm going to marry that girl!"

Uncle Tommy replied, "You're crazy, you don't even know her."

Jerry said, "I don't care. She's gonna be mine."

A few days later, Jerry approached the receptionist in my office and asked about me. They were all thrilled to give him my telephone number. What the girls in my office didn't know was that I was living in a rehabilitation center, and was only allowed two incoming calls a day for two minutes each.

Later that night, in the early morning, I was called up front and handed the phone. I recognized a strong New York accent that said, "I hope you don't mind, but I just have to get to know you."

"If you think you can do that in two minutes, fine." I responded. "If not, I'll have to call you back." I did call him back, and it seemed like we hit it off immediately. We talked for an hour. While on the phone, we made arrangements for a date after one of my half days at work.

On Thursday, the day of our date, I got all spiffed up with one of my favorite black pantsuits, high black heels, and a black beret. We decided to meet at a Chinese restaurant in the mall. Being the first to arrive, I had a seat at the bar and ordered a carafe of wine, ignoring the rehab center rules. A few minutes later, Jerry walks in all smiles, kisses me on the cheek, looks me in the eyes, and tells me I'm gorgeous. I offer him a glass of wine, and he refuses, telling me it makes him violent. Being a large, stocky guy, I really didn't want any violence in my life.

I finished the wine, and we left. When I asked him what he did for a living, he said he owned a large produce company. My mind ran back to what my doctor at work told me a few days earlier. Colombo was a mobster name from New York. However, curiosity led me to be open to him. He, knowing I lived in a rehab center, and I, knowing he was really a mobster. It seemed we were drawn to each other out of curiosity. Go figure!

We drove a little way to Daytona Beach and pulled up to the back of a hotel. Jerry tells me he has some business to take care of. We entered through the kitchen, into what looked like the manager's office. It was empty. Jerry went around and sat at the manager's desk, propping his feet up. When the manager came in and saw Jerry, he looked frightened. They shook hands, and kissed each other on the cheek with an Italian greeting. That's when Jerry told him that he'd been hearing things he didn't like. He says, "I hear you've been telling people I'm selling stolen produce?" Jerry bellows out, "Whatsa matta whichya?!" The guy stood, defending himself, and that's when I excused myself to the ladies' room.

When I returned, they were shaking hands and patting each other on the back. I was so thankful, as I didn't need anymore trouble, having already broken the rehab center's rules by drinking. I had an eerie sense that I was entering a world I had only heard about and seen in the movies.

Next, we arrived at a beautiful house on the water, because he wanted me to meet his Uncle Sal. Uncle Sal was an old man, very charming, and handsome. He offered me some wine, which I accepted very readily. I walked over to a giant window and looked out over the beautiful view, while Jerry and Uncle Sal sat and talked. In a few minutes, it was time to go eat and get me back to the center, before my curfew was over.

We went to an Italian restaurant on the Daytona Beach strip, owned by an Uncle Tommy. Neither of these two men were Jerry's real uncles, but he called them that out of a relationship of respect.

We were seated, and Jerry made sure his back wasn't facing the window, because a friend of his was gunned down in New York when his back was exposed to the street. With that knowledge, Jerry proceeded to seat me in the chair with my back to the window! *Hey, this is our first date! I've never really thought of myself as a bullet buffer, until now.* I knew I had made a small entrance into the underworld. It was exciting at that time in my life, yet creepy at the same time. We had a wonderful dinner and with the alluring atmosphere, Jerry and I seemed to be in love after only a few hours.

The next time we went out, Jerry took me to his home by the ocean. The sunset off the ocean was breathtaking! He cooked me a wonderful meal using his special sauce. It was very impressive, especially for a girl who had never really had to cook. Later on, when Jerry returned me back to the rehab center, the officials said they were putting me on restriction for being late and for smelling like wine. I called Jerry and told him I couldn't see him anymore. He told me to pack up, and he would be there to get me in twenty minutes. He assured me not to worry, that he would take care of everything. Sure enough, Jerry arrived in twenty minutes, and we headed out in his big, black van.

Even though we had only been together a short time, I was attracted to this big Sicilian with piercing green eyes. He was a take charge kind of guy. Jerry had an outgoing personality and was easy to like. He made me feel comfortable and secure, the way no other man had made me feel. His physical size, mannerisms, and self-assuredness seemed to capture my heart and soul from the very beginning of our relationship.

Jerry had a lawyer make a court date, and the judge placed me on twelve months' probation. I began to see how things got fixed by the mob. Jerry and I started living together.

A few days later, I went into the spare bedroom where my belongings were. I noticed the photos I had of me and the retired FBI agent, along with my address book, were gone! When I asked Jerry about this, he was surprised. His comment was, "You don't need any of those things. You have me now!" A red flag should have gone up right then, spelling out the words *control freak* in big, bold letters. No flags, however, for I really was in love. As far as Tony, the FBI Agent, I couldn't really end that relationship, since I didn't have his number. I'm sure he got the message though.

After Jerry and I lived together for a couple of weeks, I met his mother and two younger brothers. They were all nice and kind, expressing a sincere liking to me. There was still Pa Colombo to meet. Later in the week, we drove out to the compound that the Colombo family had built. The Italian Villa was quite impressive with its exquisite marblework inside and out. It reminded me more of a museum than a house.

The odd thing about the visit was that I was not to mention to Mr. Colombo that I had seen his home, since he wasn't there at the time. I surely didn't want to go against family tradition, so we made plans to return when his father was there.

On our next trip to the Colombo compound, Jerry felt like he had to prep me on things to do and not to do. I had to dress a certain way, not ask too many questions, and not let on, by any means, that I had already been there. I was to be introduced, sit, and sip espresso. Boy, I just couldn't wait! I had to put on an act of *oohing* and *aahhing* whenever I was shown the house by the family.

After a few Sunday visits with the family, I refused to be told I couldn't smoke before I arrived at the villa. I wasn't allowed to smell like cigarette smoke, either. Well, I lit up before arriving and had a good, rebellious smoke. Mints and spray didn't cover up the nicotine smell on me. Pa Colombo didn't think it was cute.

Mr. Colombo, being the mafia gentleman that he was, spoke in Italian and was basically telling everyone in the family that I was not welcome back on the property. I pretty much picked this up when Jerry told me to get my hat. Jerry also spoke a few loud words in Italian with his mother, after which we were out of there.

As we were going out the door, Jerry changes from Italian to English and says to them, "If she is not welcome, then I'm not either." Knowing about the close bond in this family, what Jerry said seemed like a statement of finality as far as his father and mother were concerned. On the other hand, this showed me how Jerry was committed to me. Jerry's father told him that as long as I smoked, I couldn't return to the villa.

Suddenly, I blurted out, "You mean to tell me it is okay to kill people, but smoking is a no-no!?" Jerry just laughed.

Needless to say, we had some open Sundays to visit his family. However, I encouraged him to go without me. He said he wouldn't go without me and case closed. I found out later that the only way a case was closed in the family would be if somebody died or came up missing.

Several weeks later, the family spat seemed to be mended, and a little after this, Jerry asked me to marry him. He said that since he was a teenager, he knew what his wife would look like, and I fit the picture. He said he had a few trial runs with some blondes and redheads, and he was saving the best for last.

Of course, looking back on it now, I recognize a lot of the red flag warning signs that, had I known better and had I not been swept up in such a romantic idea of Jerry and I and what our life was and would continue to be like together, I probably would have seen. For example, when he refused to be seated with his back to the window on our first date, because people in his line of work could get shot. Now, I am kind of upset that I, on that first date, was the buffer between Jerry and a bullet, but I didn't really think about it at the time.

Work was always a source of contention between the two of us. When we first got together, he'd say to me, "I can go to New York and work for my uncles, Robin." Him working, where he'd work, and what he'd do was something that we argued about a lot. He always did many different things to make money, but I didn't like the inconsistency of that lifestyle. I wanted something I could count on, someone who would always bring home what was needed, and I would never have to worry. I told him he should go to New York and do that work that he talked about; I wanted the steady paycheck, the steady home life, the steady man.

Jerry was also very, very jealous. If a man even dared to speak to me and I said hello back to him, I could always count on Jerry getting upset about it, like clockwork. Depending on the circumstances, he might say to the man, "Hey, pal, keep your nose clean. Stay away from her." To me, he'd usually say something along the lines of, "Why did you say hello to him?" It was not a healthy way to have a relationship, always considering who you were talking to, what you were saying, and how it might be taken by your significant other before you even opened your mouth.

CHAPTER 4

MARRIED TO THE MOB

Jerry and I moved to Panama City, Florida, to be close to my aunts and cousins. My parents, who lived in Jacksonville, Florida, had, in fact, disowned me for the entire six months we lived there. They even told Jerry that I was dead, in their opinion. This broke my heart. I couldn't think of anything I had done to warrant this rejection at the time. In the past, I could have seen it for some of the stupid things I had done. Maybe they thought I was rejecting them by moving away. I later found out that my aunt, my mother's sister, had had a long-standing separation over something, which caused this rejection. My parents' rejection of me brought on animosity between my parents and Jerry's parents. Oh, if only human beings could be free from so many problems and strife!

My aunt and my cousins all seemed to be pretty happy we were there. All except one cousin, who was a cop, and ran background checks on us to see if we were clean. Maybe his reason for doing this was the Colombo name. Even though he declared my shoplifting charge to my aunt and other cousin, it didn't seem to affect my relationships with them, since we were still hanging out together.

Jerry's parents came to visit us. His mother and I purchased a pregnancy test, and my test came out positive! Everyone was ecstatic—

this being their first grandchild. In 1994, Jerry and I immediately made plans to be married.   Jerry called to invite my parents to the wedding, but they refused to come. The joy of my forthcoming child and wedding were dampened by the fresh rejection by my parents. How many times can a human heart suffer hurt before it is totally crushed? I felt that my heart was near this point.

Wedding

My cousins flew in from Virginia, and all my other relatives from Panama City were very supportive of us, as well as the whole Colombo family. Our wedding was a small non-Catholic one, with neither Jerry nor me fitting the spiritual criteria of the Church. I felt like a princess, and only wished my father was there to give me away. I wanted my twelve-year-old daughter to be there as well. My parents prevented that.

You may ask why little twelve-year-old Jennifer didn't live with us? Well, my parents provided a wonderful, stable, and sheltered life for her. This fit when I was single, with the many nights I did bar work, and would also be the best for her after Jerry and I were married, as I knew we would be moving around a lot, which we soon did.

Not long after this, Jerry and I moved to Palm Coast, Florida—about an hour away from his parents. We had not been going to the family Sunday dinners, but I begged Jerry to go. They really wanted him there, although no mention was made of me. As a point of retaliation from this rejection, I made it a habit never to go on Sundays. One of Jerry's brothers left a message on our phone calling me names. Jerry heard it, and called them back. It wasn't pretty.

We had planned to name our son after Jerry's father, Francesco.

It is the Italian custom to name your firstborn son after your husband's father out of respect. I refused to name my child after a family that refused to love and respect me. So, we named our son Gennaro Colombo, Jr., leaving out his father's first name, Francesco. Our son was born May 10, 1995. What a joy this was to both of us! Not having named our son after his father was an ultimate affront, so Jerry was completely shut out of his family. When our son was two months old, I could see how much Jerry hurt from the rejection of his family. I told him I would be willing to rename our son after his father. My husband could not believe I was willing to do that for him. I told him that I loved him, and if it meant changing our son's name for him, I would do it. So, we did it!

Once again, we were getting along with both families—with mine because we moved away from Panama City and my aunt, and with Jerry's because of the name change. It's amazing how people, especially family, can so easily reject you because you don't measure up to their expectations. All that grief, strain, and pain; and for what gain? Was life to always be like this?

One particular incident from this time does stand out for me amidst the beauty and wonder of those first few years together. Growing up the way that he had, Jerry had never really had a pet. He had had 'guard dogs', working animals that served a very specific purpose, but he had never once had a pet that he could curl up with, pet, play with, and love. We decided to get a dog together. We landed on a German Shepherd, a beautiful creature with a black face that we named Bruno. Being a dog person, Jerry, of course, fell in love with him, as did I. He was such a beautiful dog, so sweet and loving. He was friendly and, like all German Shepherds, loved to play with us whenever we could.

One time, Jerry and I had to take a bit of an extended trip to New York. Unable to take Bruno with us, we decided to put him up for the duration in a doggie hotel. We thought he would be fine, and we went on our trip, confident and comfortable that our baby was in great hands. However, when we picked him up, we noticed that he was limping pretty heavily, trying to avoid putting any of his considerable weight (German Shepherds are big dogs) on one of his rear legs. After a few days of his limping with no signs of improvement, we took him to the vet in Statesboro, Georgia, one who had come highly recommended to us as "one of the best vets around". Our experience with them was quite the opposite, however. Despite Bruno's limping, they didn't even take x-rays. All they did was put an ace bandage on his rear leg, although I'm not certain what they expected that to do. Rather than a comprehensive exam of our beloved pet, they simply wrapped him up, told Jerry to bring him back in a week to remove the bandage, and sent us on our way with a hefty bill in our hands.

When we returned home, we noticed that our poor dog's paw had swelled in size, now nearly as big as a softball. Jerry immediately drove him straight back to the veterinarian, demanding that he do something further to handle our pet's issue.

The doctor, not knowing who was in his office, responded, "Well, what the f*ck do you want me to do?"

My husband, a man with a serious temper, lunged at the vet and grabbed him by the throat. Lifting him a few inches into the air, he growled, "You don't know who I am, but you damned well better find out. I'll tell you what, you're going to fix my dog's leg, or you'll end up wishing you had."

After that, Bruno and I took trip after trip, back and forth to that veterinarian's office. It was so difficult for me seeing Bruno be in so much pain and being unable to help him or to change what he was going through. On top of that, these trips were stressful on him, and, in the end, entirely superfluous. Had the veterinarian simply done his job in the first place and given Bruno the x-rays he needed, he would have discovered right away that what was affecting my dog was a condition called hip dysplasia. A painful and irreversible condition that usually affects larger dogs, my poor Bruno ended up having to have his leg amputated, because the Ace bandage the vet had applied to his leg on our first visit had been wrapped too tightly and had cut off his circulation, causing gangrene in that limb.

Because Bruno was such a large dog, the amputation ended up being too stressful on his body; he could not carry his own weight. We ended up having to put him to sleep. Although the veterinarian offered to replace Bruno with any kind of dog that I wanted, it was impossible for me. Not only did I now have a three-month-old at home to care for, Bruno was irreplaceable to us, in our hearts and in our lives. Jerry and I shed many, many tears over Bruno. We never really got over the loss of our first "baby", not either of us.

Soon, Jerry began flying back and forth to New York City. Because my husband was born into the Colombo family, born into the old school loyalty, speaking fluent Sicilian, he was moving up into the family business very quickly. On one of his trips, Jerry called me from New York. Excitedly, he told me that his Uncle Dominic set up a big deal for them. He wouldn't go into details, but he was thrilled. When Jerry returned home, he told me how he would be in charge of the McDonald's Monopoly Game, and how he would also be in charge of the big money tickets, the largest one being worth one million dollars. The next prize would be a Dodge Viper.

Next, we were off to the quaint old city of Charleston, South Carolina. We moved there because of Jerry's casino business. This wasn't the real source of my husband's income, but I never really asked him about this. Most mafia wives are kept in the dark about most things. It didn't really matter to me what Jerry did, as long as we were living in a beautiful home, driving whatever we wanted, and shopping daily. Life was good! Or so I thought! In Charleston, I decorated our beautiful, large colonial home. I had no friends, and was getting bored except for when I was with my personal trainer at the gym. Later, I found out she was Jerry's personal mistress. I was thinking a new car would make me happy. Jerry explained that the van Uncle Dominic provided for me—a nice conversion van with a TV and VCR—was perfect for my and Francesco or Frankie.

I had so little time to enjoy the van, for my husband soon got a call telling him Uncle Dominic had a heart attack while playing golf. A few days later, Uncle Dominic passed on. Little did I know that my Jerry was to replace Uncle Dominic as a boss. He would take on greater responsibilities in the business. Yet, never once did I ask what Jerry did or where the money came from.

I got bored every day and had to do something to keep me occupied or I thought that I would lose my mind. Every single day, I would take Frankie to look at houses or go shopping. I had driven to Goose Creek one day, to Crowfield Plantation, and had seen a beautiful home for sale. It was a modern home; it didn't have a fence, so I kind of eased Frankie and I around it. I really wanted to see the inside. The back of the home, what I could see, was just beautiful. It was a two-story home with a beautiful glass room in the back, the area around it all dotted with the loveliest trees. I saw the "for sale" sign and I thought *for the heck of it, let's go look in the windows.*

No one was living in the home, as far as I could tell. I saw the kitchen, and there was a huge island and a kitchenette and somewhere Frankie could sit at and eat and watch cartoons in the morning. I took down the realtor's phone number and went back home. Whenever I wanted something or Jerry wanted something, we'd call each other "Mommy" or "Daddy". When I started the conversation by saying, "Daddy", he said "Oh no."

"Daddy, there's something you have to come see with me," I told him. I didn't want him to know it was another house. I actually sold him on the place because of Frankie's safety within the cul-de-sac where it was. That's where I started trying to convince him to buy it, and I only pushed harder from there. There were five bedrooms – we would never be short on space if visitors came by. There was a spiral staircase, wasn't that gorgeous? When we went upstairs into the master bedroom, it had a big jacuzzi bathtub, and Jerry loved jacuzzi tubs. There was a huge family room over the garage, and I suggested to him that he could have his own space up there, with a leather couch and a big screen television. I made buying this beautiful house our idea, instead of just my idea, and he went with it. We had only lived in our previous house for three weeks when we decided to move.

I seemed to want more and more, but it never satisfied me. Something was always missing. I was unaware that I was slipping into depression. I could get any drug I wanted to numb the boredom. All I had to do was tell Jerry, and in about 30 minutes, it would be delivered to my doorstep and placed under the mat. I never saw who delivered it, and didn't care. My days consisted of shopping and— can you believe it? —looking for bigger homes. As a new boss, Jerry was always out of town, and I spent a lot of time alone. I couldn't even visit a friend. The closest thing I had to a friend was my hairdresser. When I jubilantly said to my husband that I was going to the beach with her, she was threatened by my husband and two of his guards.

Being very restless, it got to the point that I couldn't eat or sleep, and I began to sleep in the guest room. One night, I left my room to check on Frankie, and overheard Jerry in the other room, talking on the phone about sex. I barged into the room, and grabbed the phone. It was then that I discovered that it was my former personal trainer. They both swore they were not having an affair. I was completely distraught! All I did was cry and take sleeping pills to sleep. Anguish gripped my heart.

They had met because, wanting to work off the baby fat that I still had lingering on my body from carrying Frankie, I had decided to sign up for a gym and try to put the work in to get back to being more comfortable with my body. Of course, I couldn't just join any gym, not being with Jerry. He searched around until he found an all-women's gym, where the chances of me running into, interacting with, or talking to men would not be a problem. Before I was allowed to go to the gym – indeed, before he even paid for the membership – Jerry had demanded that he be given a tour of the entire facility, so that he could see for himself that there were no men in the vicinity. The woman that gave him that tour ended up in the position of being my personal trainer.

Of course, I had had absolutely no idea that they had been seeing each other until the night that I walked by and overheard their dirty little conversation. After grabbing the phone out of his hand and losing it on Jerry, I called my trainer, herself, and asked her, point-blank, if she was sleeping with my husband. She was cagey and elusive, telling me that I was barking up the wrong tree. I didn't really think that I was, however, and I told her so. Jerry insisted that I was mistaken, that they had just been talking about business. Of course, he had also tried to cover up his affair right before I grabbed the phone away from him by telling me that he was only on the phone with my cousin – not a great lie, either, because who would talk to their wife's cousin like that?

The "business" that Jerry was telling me that they were talking about was a movie. These people had so many connections that it made sense that they had some connections in the movie world. At that point, Jerry was supposed to be in a movie, but we had our terrible accident before that ever happened, so it never materialized into anything. By the time that I finally caught them red-handed in their affair, I think that they had been seeing each other behind my back for about a year, or maybe a little more. Besides being my personal trainer, Jerry had also given her a job at the casino. I just couldn't win in that situation. I just couldn't.

The stress of finding out about the affair put an insane amount of strain on not only my marriage, but on me personally. My depression, which had been creeping around the edges for a while, fully reared its ugly head and began to truly ruin my life. I couldn't sleep – I have always reacted to stress with bouts of insomnia – and I couldn't bring myself to eat. My weight dropped to only 115 pounds – there went that baby fat I'd been trying so hard to lose! – and I was doubting myself and my conviction about the affair every single day. Jerry had such a way about him that even if you were absolutely positive that you knew what the truth was, you would find yourself questioning your own mind every single moment. His truth was the truth, even if it wasn't the actual truth.

Jerry and his family were so worried about me that they sent me to a psychiatrist. When Jerry was told I wanted a divorce, Jerry had my cousin Teresa fly in from Virginia and my best friend, Gloria, flown in from Jacksonville. My husband took us all over downtown, shopping all day. We were to get whatever we wanted, whatever our hearts desired, no questions asked, no matter the price. Well, after a show like that, Gloria and Teresa could not believe I ever wanted to leave Jerry, my marriage, or my life. I had to remind them that what they had witnessed was not the everyday normal life for me, that it had all been a show just for them. I played along. After all, what else was there to do? They just could not understand the pain and sorrow I felt.

Finally, I began to put some trust in the doctor, and felt that someone was finally listening to and understanding me. I believed that my doctor would know how to make me feel better. He diagnosed me with depression and insomnia, and he was correct. I definitely had both. But, wait a minute! Didn't I already know these things? Weren't they obvious? We were paying him $100 an hour for putting a fancy name on stuff I already knew.

It was during a routine visit to the doctor's office one day, that really opened my eyes a little to what was going on in my life. Before going in to see the doctor, I had to go to the ladies' room. As I was walking down the hall, I looked up and saw my husband and doctor in an intense conversation. I didn't have time to think, but I went directly to where my husband was sitting and grabbed him by the throat. I must have looked like a gremlin attacking him. I remember I kept yelling at him, "You can't have this thing; this is my issue." In other words, I was telling him not to control this situation through the doctor. Jerry politely stood up and brushed me off—like a fly.

The doctor very sweetly said to me, as if I were a child, "Robin, please let Jerry go and have a seat." At once, I grasped the fact that this whole thing was a joke—a real joke. Almost in horror, I realized my life was being controlled, as another prescription was written for anxiety.

My life was being more and more controlled by Jerry. I had no friends, for my activities were constantly watched by so-called protective guards, Jerry's henchmen. Now, my innermost being was starting to be controlled—my thoughts and emotions were coming under the domination of medication. Did I have a life? Was my life my own? Yet, hadn't I started giving my life over to drugs, alcohol, and men at an early age?   Hadn't I already released my mind, will, and emotions to drugs, alcohol, and men and this was just a big harvest of trouble being reaped by me?

With only fleeting thoughts of turning to God, I didn't, and I couldn't, for I did not know Him.

Still, living in denial and deception most of the time, I thought my life was the best of all lives. I had a husband who loved me and provided great security, a beautiful child and home—almost anything I wanted. Yet, the callous betrayal of my husband to another woman shattered the deceptive walls of my heart and brought my so-called ideal life to a sudden halt. I was a prisoner in spirit, soul, and body. When I married Jerry, I married the mob, which provided an environment for even more captivity to the earlier surrendered life to drugs, alcohol, and selfish men to satisfy my selfish life.

Jerry tried to comfort me through all this by asking me to go to Atlantic City, New Jersey, with him. We arrived in Jersey, were picked up at the airport by a big limousine, and whisked off to the Taj Mahal

Hotel and Casino. We immediately joined all the other VIPs of the underworld. At the casino, gamblers were throwing money around like water. They didn't work hard for it. For most of them, the money came easy, through extortion, loan-sharking, and illegal gambling.

I seemed to be caught up into the whirlwind world of my husband. With the medication and drinking, I was numbing myself to some powerful destructive forces working inside of me. I even wanted to read my astrology chart and see a "Madam Ruby" again. By allowing the stars and a hit-or-miss prognosticator to guide my life, wasn't I now quickly reverting to more control over my life by an outside influence? This is what I told myself.

You are wearied in the multitude of your counsels; Let now the astrologers, the stargazers, and the monthly prognosticators stand up and save you, from what shall come upon you...

Isaiah 47: 13

Surrounded by revelry and partying, and soothed inside by the drugs and alcohol, I was trying to create another ideal life situation. I was so blinded.

The pride of your heart has deceived you, you who dwell in the clefts of the rock, whose habitation is high; You who say in your heart, 'Who will bring me down to the ground?'

Obadiah 1:3

Jerry would order me a drink, get up and start seeing his business cronies, and then I would be left alone.   I would watch the glitzy show by myself, and then Jerry would come back and escort me to my room. The room was a fantastic suite, with living and dining areas, plush carpet with a big picture window, and gorgeous view. Unfortunately, you couldn't go out on the balcony. The doors were permanently shut, so that the big losers wouldn't end it all by jumping over the side.

Again, I was left alone by Jerry, and the door was locked for my safety. Yeah! A prisoner, again. In retaliation, I ordered bunches of food and ran up a huge tab, only to be denied the sick joy of retaliation, for the food was free anyway. I was bored and wanted to get out of there.

I was told we were going to open up a casino in Myrtle Beach, South Carolina. We had to go house hunting, so I could not wait to get there. With my heart stirred to decorate a new house, I was suddenly told plans had changed, and the casino would not open. With us, there seemed to be no settling down, no stability, and no real peace. Yet, I was a good supportive mob wife, never needing any explanations, nor asking any questions. My life consisted mainly of being left alone with my son, Frankie. I wasn't actually resigned to this way of life, for I always had hope of a better life of freedom someday.

I knew the business and lifestyle that Jerry was living was dangerous and time-consuming. Actually, since Jerry spent so much time in Atlantic City at the Casino, he appeared to be having one big party after another. The perks of his work apparently outweighed any danger he faced. Jerry found his identity in being Sicilian, from Bensonhurst, a neighborhood of Brooklyn, New York, and proud to be a Colombo. He spoke both English and Sicilian and was very proud of his whole heritage. This heritage was from the famous Joe Colombo family.

In 1960, Joe Colombo became one of the youngest bosses of

the mob, having been an enforcer for the Profaci family. In 1971, Joe Colombo was assassinated at a meeting of the Italian American League, which he had formed several years earlier. He was kept on life-support systems until 1978, when the plug was pulled.

While still living outside of Myrtle Beach, Jerry informed me one day that he would be spending a lot of time in Hilton Head, South Carolina, remodeling a casino. Little did I know that Frankie and I would hardly see him at all.

One night, I took Frankie out to eat. Afterward, I thought I'd take him shopping. On the way to the store, I was talking to my two-year-old son, as if he could understand me. I noticed a sign on the side of the road with a flashing light that read, "Coming soon, Fuzzy Bunny Nightclub." I looked over at Frankie and said, "Hey, they're opening a new club." Then, I noticed my husband standing around with a bunch of guys in a parking lot. He was supposed to be in Hilton Head, yet, he was right here in town! A little way down the road, I found a place to turn around, and the next thing I knew, my Explorer was flying over the curb in the parking lot of the Fuzzy Bunny place. By the time I arrived at the place, my husband had gone inside. I ran inside searching for him, and spotted him sitting on a barstool, talking on his cell phone. I stormed up to him and surprised him with a punch in the face. I ran back to my truck, and Jerry ran to my side, trying to explain things to me. I was so upset that I couldn't even cry. I was in shock about catching Jerry in another big lie.

He and I started yelling at each other and creating quite a scene. About thirty guys were standing all around watching intently. I began to threaten my husband with the FBI and blurted out, "You're going down!" Then, I crazily pointed to the gang of men standing nearby and raised my voice even louder, saying, "You're all going down, too!"

Jerry and the boys weren't pleased in the least with my threats. Jerry asked me to give him Frankie. Like a fool, I did, and drove off.

Now, what was I to do? I'd better call Mom. So, I pulled over to a pay phone to call her collect. I told her, in a rushed and panicky voice, to take two names down, and if she didn't hear from me in two days, to call the feds and give them these names.

She replied, "Oh my God, Robin, what have you done?"

I told her, "Oh, nothing. I just threatened Jerry and about 30 of his goons with the FBI." After hanging up, I sat seething mad in my truck, wondering what to do and thinking about what I had just done. *Real smart move!* I said to myself. I had just threatened my husband, handed over my son, and scared my mother and father. I seemed to be making one dumb decision after another.

I really didn't want to threaten the mob, and I knew well enough that it was Jerry, and Jerry alone, that saved me from being conveniently removed from this life. Being a mafia wife, you heard stories of reprisals of murders with no names mentioned and other paybacks. I heard one story, from my mother-in-law, which happened in Sicily. Two thugs stole her brother's Mercedes Benz. The word got out on whose car it was and to return it immediately. The car was promptly returned with $20,000 cash under the front seat. What an expensive one-night joyride in a luxury car!

I drove home and found my husband there, before I arrived. I took a deep breath, went inside, and immediately saw two of Jerry's goons sitting on my couch. All 5'1", 115 pounds of me yelled at these two monsters to "Get the hell out of my house!" They didn't even blink. I left in a huff for my bedroom, and being emotionally drained of all the night's happenings, I just wanted to go to bed. Jerry came into the bedroom, and he tried again to explain why he was opening a nude bar. I knew he wouldn't control himself with the employees, if he couldn't control himself with one sports trainer. I felt so down and out!

Not wanting to hear anymore lies, I told Jerry that I wanted some money for a moving truck, so I could leave. He had ruined the city of Charleston for me—too many painful memories. All I wanted was to get out.

Two days passed and no van. Jerry and one of his goons were standing on the front porch, and I asked, "Where's the truck?" Jerry laughed and hit the big goon on the arm and said, "Ha, she thinks she's leaving!"

So, the next couple of days, I slept with my son in his room. Frankie, at two-and-a-half, didn't have a clue as to what was going on, but he loved that I was sleeping with him. I waited until Frankie fell asleep and then cried myself to sleep. My heart was so broken, yet I still did not turn to God.

One morning, shortly thereafter, I asked Jerry about the van once more and got the same laugh and response. Then, I reminded him that I wanted a divorce. He looked me straight in the eyes and said I was crazy. He said there would be no divorce. We did agree that he would give me some money, so Frankie and I could go live with my parents in Jacksonville, Florida.

After all Jerry did, I still loved him very much. In many ways, he was caring, protective of me and my son, and provided the financial security that most women would want. He really had a good personality, but when any person or situation would threaten his Sicilian, Colombo identity, a dark side of him quickly manifested. I surely didn't want anyone else to raise my son but me. Even though my parents had been good to my daughter, I wished that I could have raised Jennifer.

Jerry was now flying around everywhere taking care of the new McDonald's Monopoly game winners. The way this scam worked was that there were stickers on the sides of the McDonald's cartons. The mafia got to choose 70 of the lower employees of the company and set them up as winners. As mentioned before, the big money prize was a million dollars, and the next a Dodge Viper. Then, there were the lesser money prizes. None of the top officials of McDonald's were involved.

Every several weeks, whenever Jerry was back home in Charleston, we would meet up in Savannah, Georgia, about halfway up to Charleston from Jacksonville. We would get a nice hotel there and spend some good days together as a family, just relaxing. During these times, I would think over what had happened the past several months to damage our relationship. Even with my husband lying next to me on the bed, I felt alone and empty inside. What was I to do? I couldn't get a paying job and be on my own. It was forbidden!

One morning, on one of our family visits to Savannah, I told Jerry I just couldn't live like this anymore. We had to go our separate ways. He again reminded me there was to be no divorce. Next thing I know, Jerry had a pillow over my face, and Frankie started crying. Jerry said he would chop me into little pieces, or tie me up somewhere, feed me enough to keep me alive, and tell my parents I was hooked on drugs. There was something different in his voice— it was very alarming. I knew he meant what he said. In a flash, Jerry dialed his cell phone and yelled, "Code red, code red!" The next thing I knew, he was letting his goons in and telling them I wasn't to leave!

I was in a daze at this point. I couldn't believe what was happening. My son and I were virtually prisoners of the mob, as these goons kept their eyes intently on us. They left us, and a few minutes later, I noticed that the door of the hotel room was partially open. I rushed out the door and passed through the door of another room and saw a cleaning maid. I yelled out to her, "Quick, call 911!"

She threw her arms up and screamed, "Holy Jesus!" She ran right by me and Frankie.

Next, I ran to the end of the balcony and yelled out to a huge man down below, "Help!" He looked over my head and said he wasn't going to get involved. *Geez!! Is anyone going to help me?* Immediately, I ran down the stairs, where Frankie and I got into my truck. Wouldn't you know it, no keys! Jerry and his goons gave chase and trapped me in my truck. I blurted out, "Just give me the keys. I just want to leave." I also told them they had better leave, because I was sure the police were on their way—I really didn't know this. Now, Jerry wanted to talk things over. I told him, "I don't think so." Saints alive, the police did show up! I got my keys and the police placed Jerry in the back of their car to question him and the goons.

When they asked me what I wanted to do, I told them all I wanted to do was to go back to my parent's home in Jacksonville. They released my husband, and we all left separately—Jerry going north, and Frankie and I heading south. I cried all the way home, while Frankie slept.

A few weeks passed, and we were on speaking terms again. Jerry told me he would do anything to keep our family together. He promised things would change and he would slow down in his work.

There was still a lot of pressure on Jerry to finish up the McDonald's Monopoly Game. It was May 6, 1998, when he finished with the Monopoly thing—everything was called the *thing*. He flew in and picked up Frankie and me at my parent's house, and we traveled up to Georgia, hoping to find some property to build on. We agreed to look for some land at the last exit in Georgia, before reaching the South Carolina border. We compromised on where we would be living. I would only be about two

hours away from my family in Jacksonville, and he could commute to Hilton Head, South Carolina, where the casino was. Maybe our lives could take on some semblance of peace this way. There was to be no peace, as the next event in our lives brought only more pain and misery.

CHAPTER 5

THE MONOPOLY THING

When it came to Jerry's business and the work that he did, there were a lot of things I begged him not to tell me anything about. I know that I lived off of a lot of the money that we got from these things, but I didn't want to get involved with anything he did. I knew some of it was bad. On top of that, truth be told, I'm not a very good liar. Had anyone ever asked me about any of it, the truth of it would have been written all over my face. However, just because that was the way that it had always been didn't mean that that was the way it would stay.

He was the number two man in the Monopoly thing, and I was his right hand on that, because in my opinion, no one was getting hurt. It was, to me, essentially a victimless crime. I always asked Jerry, when it came to his business, to please never hurt anyone. As far as I could see, the Monopoly thing followed that request of mine just fine. Some people would win some money, we would make something from it, no one got hurt. It didn't even really feel like an actual crime. McDonald's was giving away the money anyways; we were just navigating the winners.

I had only had fringe knowledge of what he did before that. I knew that he and the people he worked with were in the football gambling business. My husband and his crew would fly to Atlantic

City every two weeks. He and his crew were treated like kings at the Taj Mahal; whenever they would arrive, the proverbial red carpet would be rolled out from the moment that they walked off of the plane. I went with him a few times; when we went, we got the red-carpet VIP treatment. The pit bosses in the casino all knew my husband, of course. We stayed in suites where the bedroom had elephant tusks around the bed, there was a button you could push and the television came out of the floor, all of the bathrooms had gold faucets, and there was gorgeous, buttery-soft leather furniture in the living room.

We didn't have to pay for anything, because of who they were and how much business Jerry and his men brought in. They didn't hang around low-life people; they hung around politicians, actors, and people of wealth. We had a Corvette that we received as payment from a well-known singer because he owed the mob some money. Instead of paying the money, he gave Jerry his car. We drove the Corvette around for a while, but it wasn't for our entertainment, it was for my husband to blow up and get the insurance money on it. I told him I couldn't be around for that bit; he took me to a hotel so I could wait, instead.

We had our own casino in Charleston, called the Golden Monkey. In addition to the Monkey, Jerry also had an underground casino in Hilton Head. It was a key club – you had to have a key to get into it. It cost a lot of money to have that key, and very few people had it who weren't practically dripping in wealth. Uncle Dominic - who was a godfather - was partners with Uncle Jerry. Uncle Dominic had a heart attack on the golf course in Hilton Head. When he died, there were so many politicians and rich people that he had been involved with, their business sort of just trickled down to us. I knew they were also involved in loan sharking, though that was something I definitely didn't want to know about, because I knew people probably got hurt if they couldn't pay what they owed. Lastly, there was the Fuzzy Bunny strip club, which I stayed away from one hundred percent for obvious reasons.

In 1995, when Jerry called me from New York about the Monopoly gig, he explained to me over the phone that Uncle Dominic, the Godfather, had hooked him up with the head of the winners of the Monopoly game pieces, and his part in all of it would be to recruit big winners—anything over $100,000. He was very excited about the Monopoly job, because it meant there would be more money annually. He was more excited about it than I was at first. He saw the long-term vision of it. He brought it to me as "we'll be set for life," and I didn't see that, but then as the tickets started coming in, I started seeing just how big it was. So, for Uncle Dominic to give my husband the opportunity to even meet Uncle Jerry, who provided the Monopoly game pieces, and to work with him on this big, big job, showed how much Jerry was trusted. You see, my husband was full-blooded Sicilian. He spoke the language fluently, and he had old school ways. Being trusted, being in the confidence of these powerful people, showed him that everything that he had done up to that point had been worth it. He was in, he was officially one of the family, he had done enough right things to be a part of something huge.

The steps my husband had to take to do his part in the Monopoly thing were to fly to the Atlanta airport and meet with Uncle Jerry. Uncle Jerry would then tell him what city and state in which the winning McDonald's ticket was to be won at. Then, they would go to the men's restroom and make the exchange. My husband would wrap the winning ticket up in tissue paper, put it away, fly back home with it, and show it to me when he got there. I can remember him asking me if I wanted to see what a million-dollar game piece looked like, and he would unwrap the tissue paper, and there it would be, nestled in all of that white paper: a one-million-dollar monopoly game piece. It seemed wild to me that one million dollars could look like that colorful little slip of paper. The reason the men's bathroom was chosen for their meeting place was because there were no cameras, so no one would have any record of what they were up to. Besides, who would question two men going into a bathroom at a busy airport? I suppose I should have been, or could have been, worried about all of it – how it would affect my family, my life, my marriage – but I simply wasn't. It still seemed so innocent to me, and I truly believed that no one was getting hurt. I went pretty much all in with Jerry.

As far as I know, at the beginning it was Uncle Jerry, my husband, and I who were involved with working on the Monopoly thing, recruiting the winners. The winners absolutely knew what they were getting into, because they had to pay for the ticket, and then they would have to go to the McDonald's where the ticket was to be found, because that was pre-recorded. I was the one who got Gloria, my best friend, involved. I called her up on the phone, explaining to her how the Monopoly game worked, what she would have to pay to get the million-dollar ticket, and what she would receive annually, which was $50,000 for twenty years – it was that or a huge lump sum of money, which would be very heavily taxed, so the slower payments seemed like a better choice. I got her involved from the other side of it too, explaining to my husband that they needed a woman, especially a woman of color, to win, because at that point, they were only having men as winners, when mostly women were the ones who would go to McDonald's. Finally, they agreed to let Gloria be a winner. I was thrilled. Simon Marketing in Chicago – with whom Uncle Jerry worked – was so pleased that a woman of color had won, they flew her up to Chicago and gave her this large banquet where Sherman Hemsley picked her up in a limousine at the Four Seasons Hotel. They treated her like a queen. At first, she was very excited about the idea. I was very excited about the idea of giving my best friend a million-dollar ticket and to be able to give my family members the tickets as well. My opinion was that obviously someone had to win, and they all went to McDonald's, so why not them? Why not the people that I loved and cared about, people who I knew needed the money and would use it well?

We would find a person, and that person would pay for the winning ticket. They paid $100,000 for the ticket, knowing that they'd be getting much more in return when they won. The security team that ran the game for McDonald's, Simon Marketing, would predetermine the location of the McDonald's where each ticket would be won. The person who bought the game piece from us had to go to the city with the certain McDonald's and redeem the ticket. Once the ticket was authenticated, McDonald's corporate would be in touch with the winners, because they usually wanted them to do a commercial, although I know my dad and my best friend never wanted to do that. My husband had a CPA who was supposed to win the $50,000 ticket, but he had backed out at the last minute because buying the ticket in the first place wasn't feasible for him in his tax bracket. Gennaro ended up having to redeem the ticket himself at a McDonald's in Brooklyn. He even appeared in a commercial, and when I saw it, I laughed out loud, because he was such a ham.

One of the other winners of the Monopoly thing was my father. I'll never forget it, because my dad breaking the law was astonishing in and of itself, and him asking me to help him blew me away. I had always felt like the black sheep of the family, and my father had never asked me for anything before in my life. When he called, I was in my bedroom in Charleston. The cordless phone was laying on my bed, and I picked it up. My dad, after asking how we were doing and making a few minutes of small talk, said, "Robin, I want the big one." I was absolutely flabbergasted. Afterward, I didn't even get bragging rights that Dad had asked me for something, because no one could know that he had come to me, or that I had been a part of any of it. I wanted to be able to brag so badly that he had come to me for something, because I was had been put down by my brother and sister my whole life, and it had always felt awful, like I didn't meet the expectations that my father had for me and therefore didn't meet the family standards. Apparently, my husband had asked my dad about the Monopoly thing, and I didn't know about it until sometime afterwards.

When Jerry told me, I said to him, "You don't go to my family, you leave them out of all of this. My family doesn't do this stuff."

Jerry told me, "Quit worrying about it, Robin, he said no anyway."

I don't know how much time passed between Jerry asking my dad and my dad asking me, although I would probably say that at least a year had gone by. The million-dollar ticket was supposed to be my winning ticket, but I gave it to my dad, instead. Jerry asked if I was sure, and I told him, "He must really need it, or he wouldn't have come to me. He doesn't come to me for anything, and he doesn't break the law." I never saw Jerry give the ticket to my father, but I know my dad only paid $60,000 for it—even though most people had to pay $100,000—because he was family. The two of them took a road trip to Boston, where the ticket had to be won. I didn't go to that; I stayed home and waited patiently for the news to come out that another winner had been found. I never participated in the trips where Jerry would take people to the McDonald's stores, and this time was no exception, even though I was happy for my dad. I don't know what my dad ended up doing with all of the money he won. I think he most likely invested some. Like I said, he must have really needed it for him to even ask. He was a very prideful man. I know that took a lot out of him. I'm sure he lost a lot of sleep over that one.

The Monopoly thing went on for a long time. It wasn't a short or fast thing; it was a long game. I think the total ended up being twelve years, all told, that they chose who would win and got their cuts of the winnings. In the end, the amount that the rigged winners received was more than twenty million dollars. Mostly, Jerry and I found people who could be trusted with what was going on – although Jerry did most of it, meeting with them, taking them to the McDonald's, all of that. My part officially ended in 1998, after Jerry died. I wanted to leave the mob life behind and start a new life for myself and my son.

I was hated by a lot of my family members when this all came to an end. I carried the blame and rightly so, because in fact, I knew about this, and had participated. A lot of people looked down on me for bringing my father into it, but I loved him that much, he was worth every penny of a million dollars to me and much more. I felt my heart was in the right place by giving my family members and friends winning Monopoly game pieces. Someone had to win, so why not them? Why not the people I knew for sure deserved it? If people were just a little more honest with themselves, maybe not all people, but quite a few, would love the opportunity to have the chance to give friends and family a million dollars. They probably would have done the same thing that I did. But of course, all of my best intentions meant nothing once the feds got involved and the Attorney General— which was John Ashcroft at the time— turned our world upside down.

CHAPTER 6

AN EMOTIONAL AFFAIR

When you are in a marriage that is as tumultuous and painful as the marriage I had with Jerry, sometimes you find yourself looking for love – and validation, and affection, and someone to tell you that you are perfect – in a place that is not located within the confines of your relationship. What I did, what I felt I needed to do to find myself again and assert that I was a person outside of simply being a mother to Frankie and a wife to Jerry, was not the most perfect decision I have ever made. But I am a human woman, and I was suffering under the strain of a happy marriage gone terribly, terribly wrong. I loved Jerry, but there were so many aspects of who he was and who we were together that erased me from the narrative of our marriage entirely. I wanted to feel alive again. I wanted to feel beautiful, wanted, sexy, desirable. I wanted to see who I might have been if I had not entered into my marriage.

So, I found myself, somewhat unknowingly at first, reaching out to someone that made me feel all of those things and more. I wasn't perfect and I know that, but there was a part of me that was locked away, feeling neglected and forgotten, and I began to want to nurture that part of myself with the love and affection that I felt was withering away with Jerry. I engaged in an emotional affair with one of the people that he knew and trusted the most. Because Jerry knew and trusted him implicitly, I did as well.

The beginning of my affair was slow, very slow. You have to understand that my life, how I had lived it and the things I had worked toward, had dissipated once I married Jerry. I went from having an exciting nightlife working in a bar, one filled with people and friends and fun nights out, to doing very little outside of decorating my home again and again and shopping relentlessly for things I didn't really need. I was disappearing before my own eyes, and I didn't know how to stop that in its tracks or even slow it down. So, I reached out, searching for a person who might be able to remind me of the person I was afraid I was losing.

I was married, and I took the vows that I had made very seriously. But "Uncle Jerry", the man who controlled so much of what we said and did, had something mysterious about him that drew me to him almost against my better judgment. Uncle Jerry and my husband had met through Uncle Dominic, "the Godfather" of their family. From what I understand, Uncle Jerry and Uncle Dominic were partners. When Uncle Dominic died, Uncle Jerry stepped up and took over a lot – if not all – of the projects that they had been involved in together. The money from these "projects" was, at the time, tied up in probate after Uncle Dominic's death. Uncle Dominic had adopted children from his first wife and made them his legal children, and much of the money involved in the things that they had done was apparently going to be divided up among them. Although Uncle Dominic had not left them anything in his will, when he died, they contested the will, itself. Eventually, Uncle Jerry paid them each somewhere between $100,000 and $150,000 to go away, although I'm not entirely positive on the actual amount that it ended up being.

Anyway, at some point before his death, Uncle Dominic had introduced my Jerry and Uncle Jerry. When I first spoke to Uncle Jerry, I was in a state of extreme emotional distress over the state of my marriage. I had only recently found out about Jerry's affair with my personal trainer. I was so devastated that I couldn't eat. I had gone into a fierce depression that stole me from myself, my family, and my husband. I was crushed. I couldn't hold back the rage and despair I felt over the affair – I threatened to divorce Jerry regularly. Sometimes, I meant it, sometimes, I was speaking out of my anger, and other times, I think I wanted to see what he would say when I insisted that I wanted to end our marriage. I used the word "divorce' freely, but I really didn't want a divorce. After I would yell and scream at him, I would leave and think about being without him. I would imagine what it would really be like; how lonely it would be, how it would feel to never laugh with him or kiss him or make love to him again. It would crush me, and I'd want him to beg me to stay.

During one of these arguments, he was on the phone with Uncle Jerry. I'll never forget what happened. I was complaining to my husband, because it seemed as though I did everything around the house; I even took out the garbage and cut the grass. Our home was immaculate, thanks to my constant efforts, and it felt as though I was the only one who even cared to do any of these things. Jerry was very lazy.

"I can't believe you. You don't do shit around here to help me," I yelled.

"I work," he countered. "I bring you money."

"You hardly work! You don't even break a sweat. Roofers sweat when they work. That's real work," I threw back.

"You want me to sweat?" he demanded.

"Yeah, I want you to sweat, Jerry. You need to sweat. From work, not just from being hot."

The phone rang. Uncle Jerry was calling. Jerry told him I was busting his balls for not sweating to make a living, and Uncle Jerry told my husband to put me on the phone. When I held the phone to my ear, I heard him laughing.

"What about marrying me?" he asked. I walked away, so Jerry couldn't hear.

"I'm already married," I told him.

I began to look forward, immensely, to the phone calls from Uncle Jerry. Before long, he was calling to talk to me, not my husband. We began to speak more and more often, eventually talking to one another every single day. When you spoke to Uncle Jerry, you could feel the power that he wielded coming through the phone line. There was mystery there for me, too, with never seeing him in person and being able to build him up in my mind to be whatever I wanted him to be, whatever I needed him to be in that moment. With my struggling marriage and the constant tension between Jerry and me over everything under the sun, Uncle Jerry became my knight in shining armor. He became a respite in my confusing world, and he was a voice at the other end of the line that I could count on to be there, to talk to me as though he believed that I was a real human woman with real human feelings, and to make me feel as though I was standing under the only light in a dark room.

Asking me to marry him the first time that we spoke had not been a fluke; although I had believed that it was a set-up, something to test my loyalty to my husband, it turned out that that couldn't have been farther from the truth. After the first proposal, he asked me to marry him again, and again, and again. I always said no and laughed it off, came up with some reason or other why I had to say no – not the least of which was my actual marriage – but he kept asking, anyway. He had such an aura of confidence, of power, and I have always, my entire life, been drawn to powerful men. With power comes money, nine times out of ten, and Uncle Jerry had a lot of that, too.

He began to send me gifts. The charm and flattery of our phone calls began to leak into my everyday life. One time that I remember, he tried to send me $15,000. I was not at home to receive the money, so it ended up getting sent back, but he kept sending gifts anyway. On that particular occasion, my husband and I had been in Wilmington, North Carolina looking for a prime piece of property on which to build a new house. I couldn't move on from his affair with my personal trainer, and we ended up in a huge fight. I threatened to divorce him. As usual, he told Uncle Jerry that I was mad and wanted to leave him. The next thing I knew, Uncle Jerry was sending me $15,000 just to keep me happy.

On another instance, he was going to buy me a horse—I had always loved riding horses. I wanted something to do, something to keep me occupied and fill my days with more than spending money and incessantly decorating my home. I wanted a horse. I had found a place to buy one, and had gone to take a look at what they had. I chose a horse that I felt a connection to – it was a beautiful horse, with soulful eyes and a gorgeous mane. I kept visiting it and watching it until I made my final decision. Uncle Jerry was going to purchase it for me. He was all set to put the money down, but my husband got mad at the lady who ran the place where they sold the horses. She had told Jerry that she didn't have a horse big enough for him, and he exploded.

"Are you calling me fat?" he hollered at her.

I was mortified; Jerry was a big man. A big man needs to ride a large horse, otherwise it'll be uncomfortable for both the horse and the rider. We didn't end up getting the horse that day. Jerry had been okay with Uncle Jerry buying me a horse – he never suspected a thing. He had no clue how Uncle Jerry felt about me until later.

One of the things that was most important to me about my emotional affair with Uncle Jerry was the friendship that we had cultivated over our long hours spent talking on the phone. I said that he was my knight in shining armor, and he really was. My marriage was on the rocks. I would get enraged at Jerry and reach out to Uncle Jerry for the support that I needed. Jerry was a liar to the bone; he got so good at lying to me that I would begin to believe the lies that he would tell me, even when I knew the truth as an irrefutable fact. I needed someone to urn to when I would get sad or angry, and Uncle Jerry was always there.

The emotional affair, the more-than-friendship had been going on for quite some time. We had never actually met in person – it was a line that I was afraid to cross. I knew that a little flirting was harmless, the phone calls we had – though I never revealed the length and frequency of them to my husband – were safe, because we weren't in the same neighborhood, the same city, or even the same state. Uncle Jerry lived in Atlanta, Georgia with his wife – he was married as well. On more than one occasion, however, Uncle Jerry would ask my husband to send me to Georgia to visit him and his wife. With everything that was going on between us behind the scenes, I knew it would be a terrible idea if I went. I knew that I was still safe, as far as an actual affair was concerned, because I had not crossed the line that I had drawn in my own mind delineating what an affair actually was. Phone calls, sure, a little flirting, some suggestive things said, okay, but actually cheating? I could not bring myself to go through with it, and I knew that if I went to Atlanta, our flirting would reach another level, and we wouldn't just be "friends" anymore. I knew we might do something that we could never, ever take back. So, I refused, and I didn't go.

Whenever I would threaten to leave my husband, I would find that outrageous gifts and offers were placed in front of me. I knew that the people involved were just trying to buy me off, keep me there, but I didn't really make the emotional connection to what that meant. Once, Uncle Jerry offered to buy me a flower shop, of all things. He offered to do this in order to keep me busy and happy, give me something to do because I had never been the type of woman who was happy simply sitting on the couch and watching her son play, or shopping until my mind was numb. I refused the offer of the flower shop – what would I have done with it? I knew nothing about flowers. It was such a wild proposal. I simply could not imagine myself arranging flowers for a living and being content and happy doing it.

I never technically received many of the gifts that Uncle Jerry would send, but he would give things to my husband for him to share with me. One of the gifts that arrived for "us" was a beautiful black Cadillac. He also gave me a gorgeous white Firebird, which I did successfully receive. Unfortunately, I wrecked the Firebird. I had been told not to drive it until they put new tires on it because the tires it had were bald. In Charleston, most of the bridges have metal grates, which don't go so well with bald tires on a fancy car. Jerry was in front of me in the Lincoln, and somehow, I lost control of the Firebird. I slid, I spun around, and I smashed into the metal. That night, after the crash, Uncle Jerry called me and told me, "We can replace that, but we can't replace you." He always said all of the right things to me. Where I used to feel completely safe with my husband, I now felt that way with Uncle Jerry.

After about a year of phone calls, gifts, and other things with Uncle Jerry, my husband let me know that Uncle Jerry would be flying into Charleston for one night. Not only would he be visiting, he would be staying with us. I was excited, thrilled, and nervous, all at the same time. I couldn't believe that we were actually going to meet in person after everything that we had had going on. I had so many things to do to prepare for Uncle Jerry's visit, I didn't really even know where to start. I had to get the perfect dress, I needed to have my hair done. I had him so built up in my heart and in my mind that when the day was to come for us to finally meet in person, it was like a child waiting on Santa Claus. It seemed to take forever for the day to actually arrive.

Finally, it was real: Uncle Jerry would be visiting my home that night. After shopping in what felt like a thousand different stores, I had found the perfect red dress, sexy but classy, with a slit up the side that showed my leg. I went to the salon that day and had the hairdresser give me an updo. I had wanted it to be more up and messy, but she used a little too much hairspray. It was too late to have it changed, though, so I had to work around it, even if it didn't fit into the vision that I had of myself when I would finally meet him. Despite all of my preparation and my planning and everything I had done to be just right, when Uncle Jerry finally walked through our door, I lost all of my poise. I leapt into his arms and kissed him, not once, but twice. My two-year-old followed suit and did the same thing. Uncle Jerry felt welcomed, to say the least. He laughed and said that I looked gorgeous, that I looked like a woman straight out of Goodfellas.

We had a beautiful Italian dinner in our formal dining room. Although I don't remember the name of the dish, it was traditional and delicious. I adored the compliments Uncle Jerry was giving me, about me personally, about how I decorated our home. He leaned over to me and told me quietly that he hadn't known that I would be so beautiful. He told us how down to earth Frankie and I were, and he was kind to my son. When he first saw my home, he told me I should be an interior decorator. I always want my home to be comfortable. When a person visits my home, I want them to feel the warmth and the welcome, and that's what Uncle Jerry felt because of how I had it set up. I was positively glowing from the compliments and the praise that he was showering on me. Jerry, of course, thought nothing of it.

I had never seen what Uncle Jerry looked like. I had had no idea what to expect, except what Jerry had described to me. When I finally met him, I thought he was very handsome. He looked distinguished; he had grey hair, he was tall and slender – but not too slender. He clearly took excellent care of himself. He looked dapper in his suit – I love a man in a suit. The way he carried himself was incredibly appealing; he had a lot of class. After dinner, I left the room and put Frankie to bed, letting the men talk about their business. It had been an amazing evening, with the food and the wine and the conversation with Uncle Jerry all leaving me feeling as though I was glowing on the inside. I only wish he could have stayed longer.

I had never been afraid of Jerry finding out about my emotional affair. After all, he was so loyal to Uncle Jerry, why would he have thought anything of the gifts and the money and everything else? However, all things like that inevitably come to end, and my affair with Uncle Jerry was no exception. While visiting in Connecticut with my husband, I let the cat out of the bag, because I was pissed off. Despite my own overwhelming feelings for Uncle Jerry, it seemed to me that Jerry's loyalty was going more to Uncle Jerry than it was to me. Here I was, giving my husband 110 percent of my loyalty, never crossing a line with Uncle Jerry or allowing things to progress beyond harmless flirtation, and Jerry was paying me back for that by being more loyal to someone else. And not just someone else, the man I was having an emotional affair with!

I had never said anything about what had been going on with me and Uncle Jerry because I was honestly afraid for the safety of my husband if he were ever to find out and confront Uncle Jerry himself. Despite this, when we were in Connecticut, in a hotel, I asked him to give me his beeper code, because if he was going to listen to my messages, I was going to listen to his. He told me that before he could do anything like that, he would have to ask Uncle Jerry first. I exploded and demanded to know if he really knew who it was that he had been giving his loyalty to all of this time. When I slipped and said that, he asked me what I meant, and it was all over. I told him how Uncle Jerry had asked me to marry him and how we had been talking for ages. I told him how I felt about Uncle Jerry and what it was like to be turning to someone else for the comfort and happiness that I should have been getting from him. Shocked and angry, Jerry left the room to call Uncle Jerry. I never heard the conversation, and I don't know what they said to one another, but I know that the conversation didn't end up going Jerry's way.

The emotional affair with Uncle Jerry ended that night. There were no more phone calls between us, no more flirtations, no more gifts that were obviously meant for me. We would speak now and again when he called to speak to my husband, but the conversations were always short and sweet. He would ask me how I was, but little else other than to ask if "the big guy" was home. I would hand the phone to Jerry without another word, feeling sad that whatever had been there was now lost. I didn't want to leave my husband, and I wouldn't have gone any farther with Uncle Jerry than phone calls and flirting, but it still felt as though something special in my life, something that was mine and mine alone, was gone, and that was a harder pill to swallow than I had thought that it would be.

Despite what had happened with Uncle Jerry, my husband, Jerry, was really my soulmate. If I had it all to do again, if I was given the opportunity to make different choices about my life, I would still marry him all over again. I wasn't on the right medication for my Bipolar I at the time that we were together, and I know how much that contributed to the problems that we had with one another. I wish now that I would have been in better condition for him—he put up with a lot from me, but never laid a hand on me. It wasn't a happy marriage, but there was a lot of love in it. Still, sometimes I wonder what might have been different if I had chosen Uncle Jerry.

After my husband died, someone else took over the McDonald's thing, and I didn't talk to Uncle Jerry anymore. I wonder now, though, what we might have said if we had spoken, if we had stayed in touch after the car crash and after everything. I suppose I won't ever find out, not now.

CHAPTER 7

FATAL CRASH

On May 7, while driving in southern Georgia up to South Carolina, Jerry kept getting calls from his mother trying to page him. I asked several times if he was going to call her, and he replied he would do so when he got home. Frankie's birthday was the tenth of May, and that day also fell on Mother's Day. Jerry's pager rang again, and it was his attorney calling to finalize plans for Jerry to study a script for a movie he was to film in Hollywood, California.

As we drove on, we were all getting a little irritable, so we stopped to have a nice steak dinner. Jerry was in a real foul mood, but apologized saying, "It's rough being around a lot of people in New York City." After the meal, we got back on the expressway and decided to rent a house in Savannah, until we found the right spot to build on. Jerry was really tired, so I did the driving.

The next few moments of our lives happened in the fastest blur, but when I remember them now, it's almost as though I see them in slow motion, moving carefully across my memory as I try to piece together every second. We had left the restaurant and were headed back home. As we came up to the expressway entrance, I pulled up next to a semi-tractor trailer. The massive truck was to the right of me at the yield sign, but I didn't think that anything was out of the ordinary – after all, people pull up next to giant trucks on the expressway all of the time. I gently but firmly tapped the brakes and didn't see anyone coming when I looked in both directions – as much as I could see around the truck, I didn't see anyone heading my way. As I was pulling across the road to go and get onto the expressway, I felt a tremendous jolt; it felt as though a huge creature had pushed our car up from the ground on the passenger side. Even though I had looked, even though I had slowed down, we were T-boned by another semi-truck. The sound was terrible, and the feeling was even worse. The huge vehicle pushed us 250 yards and slammed us up against a concrete wall, with Jerry receiving the first impact because of where he was seated in the car. The next thing I remember, I was waking up, slowly and groggily, my mind fuzzy and not fully understanding what was happening. A policeman and a paramedic were leaning above me, talking to me and telling me to remain as still as I possibly could. I could see, out of the edges of my eyes, that I was covered with blood. I could hear a terrible high-pitched whining noise, which I only learned later was the sound of the saw as they cut me out of the car, so that they could get me to the hospital. When they finally were able to get me free, Frankie and I were put into an ambulance\ together, and Jerry was flown in a helicopter to the trauma center in Savannah by Life-Flight. With my son next to me, I knew he was okay, but I didn't have or receive any information on Jerry, his injuries, or what his condition might be. I wracked my brain to determine if he was going to be alright, and all I could remember was that after the crash, he had had no blood on him whatsoever. He was in the passenger seat when we were hit, but he had been able to crawl through from the front of the car to the back of it, and get outside. I was the one crushed against the concrete wall, covered with my own blood and rendered unconscious.

In the ambulance, the paramedics had acted immediately to address my injuries, and had strapped me down, so that I couldn't have moved a muscle, even if I had wanted to. I wasn't unconscious anymore, however, and I could feel the tremendous pain shooting through my entire body as we drove to the hospital. Every bump on the road, every turn that the ambulance made, was sheer agony for me. It seemed to take longer than anything else ever had, but eventually, we arrived at the hospital.

When we got there, they rushed me to the emergency room. While I was there, I could hear the sound of my husband screaming from down the hall. Terrified that something was happening and that I couldn't see what it was, I asked the people around me repeatedly what was happening to him. They reassured me, over and over again, that he was going to be just fine. They insisted that the only things that were wrong with him were that he had a broken hip and a busted leg. I felt such a great relief wash over me at those words; I suppose that I needed to believe that Jerry was fine, that nothing was so very wrong with any of us, and that we had gotten out of that horrible crash with little more than wounds that could be stitched up, set straight, and repaired by the doctors and nurses in the emergency room. However, when I looked up next, I noticed that a priest and a nun were in the area, and my mind clouded with fear once again. Were things that serious with us, that they needed to call in a priest and a nun? Was someone, one of the members of my family, in such dire straits that they would need their last rites? I began to panic that the crash and the resulting injuries were far more serious that I was being told, but once again, the doctors and nurses assured me that everyone was just fine. I felt a cold horror creep through my veins; if

Jerry was okay, like they kept telling me, and my son was alright, as I knew he was from riding in the ambulance with him, then it must have been me who was dying. I felt so much pain, and I knew that it was bad, but was it bad enough that I could actually die? Would lying on this emergency room table be the very last thing I would ever do?

A short while later, when they had handled the worst of what was wrong with me, they cut the clothes I had been wearing off of me and began to shuttle me back and forth for X-rays and CT scans. They came to prep me for surgery, because, after having been checked out several times by many doctors, they had determined that my heart and my liver were damaged somehow, and that they would have to put me under and cut me open to determine what could be done next. However, after this had been going on for two days, everyone going back and forth on whether or not I would need surgery, the doctors decided that I did not need any surgery after all. They couldn't decide exactly what had happened, but looking back now, I know it must have been the divine and beautiful will of God that I was saved. At the time, of course, I did not know Him yet, so I did not know to thank him. Instead, I turned my concern and panic from my own condition to that of my husband, and began to wait and see what was going to happen next. It was obvious to me by then that Jerry did not, in fact, have simply a broken leg and broken hip. He was still in the hospital, he was still suffering, and they were trying to figure out what to do.

He was too big to get into the machine for a CT scan. Once they realized this, they decided they were going to do exploratory surgery on him, but his blood pressure had dropped so low by the time they could, they told us that he wouldn't survive the tremendous stress on the body that surgery causes. Instead, they chose to put him in a medical coma in the intensive care unit of the hospital. He had become so sick that he had begun having a fever, and that fever had gotten so high that they covered him with a refrigerated blanket to try to keep his body temperature within a safe range, if they couldn't get it back to a normal one.

When both of our families arrived at the hospital, my mother-in-law ran over to me and told me that she had known that this was going to happen. She had had a vision in a dream the night before; in her dream, she had seen the entire accident, and she had also had a vision of her own deceased mother. She told me that that was why she had been trying to page Jerry all day on the day of the accident. He, of course, had ignored every one of her pages, reasoning that he would get back to her when he had more time and we weren't on the road. She had wanted to warn him about the dream and tell him not to go out on the road. At the time that I saw her, I still   did not know the seriousness of my husband's condition. I was unprepared to see Jerry just lying there motionless, with his eyes closed. I stood up and shook his arm and begged him to wake up.

A week later, after I was mobile and they had released me from the intensive care unit and put me into my own room, I insisted that they take me to go see my husband. I needed to see him; I needed to know what was going on. When I walked into his room, I experienced a shock like none I had ever had before. I was completely and entirely unprepared to see my big, strong husband, a man who had been so full of life, who talked so loud and made decisions and jokes so easily simply lying there motionless on a hospital bed, hooked up to tubes and machines and who knows what else. Time seemed to stop when I saw him, but I quickly came back to myself, rushing over to the side of his bed and trying to get him to wake up. I just grabbed his arm and said, "Daddy, Daddy, it's Mommy, wake up!" He opened his eyes, a few shining tears coming out the sides and making tracks down his cheeks, and, then, he closed them again.

A few days later, the strangest thing happened when we were all in the waiting room at the hospital, listening to the doctor and trying to make some sense out of what was going on. My son walked up to the doctor and asked if he was the one who made his Mommy better. The doctor replied, "No, it was your Mommy who made herself better."

My family and I went into the chapel to pray. I can't remember what I asked for or what I said when I prayed, but I know that Frankie asked God to make his Daddy better. I didn't know what to say when he asked for that great gift. Later, the doctor told me that Jerry would have to die to get better. Those words were a shock; to say that someone need to die in order to improve means that the condition that they are in must be very grave. I had no idea how to respond.

One week after the accident, I was released from the hospital, and I went to Jacksonville with my parents to try to heal and wait for whatever Jerry's diagnosis was going to be. We drove back and forth from Jacksonville to the hospital almost constantly; I was nowhere near as mobile as I wanted to be, but I had to see Jerry, to know what was happening, to be there when he woke up. Not long after, I heard the phone ring. I don't remember now if I felt it in my body or not, that something bad was about to happen. It was the hospital, calling to tell me that Jerry was not improving. In fact, he was getting worse. I began to fall apart; if I had known that when I went to his room, it would be the last time I would ever see him open his eyes, I might have said or done something differently, although I had no idea what that might have been. And then, two weeks after the accident, all life support for Jerry was terminated.

I lost it when I found out that Jerry was gone. I fell to the floor, crying, screaming his name over and over again. I didn't want to live any more. I didn't know how I would go on without him. At the time of making funeral arrangements for Jerry, I was approaching my 36th birthday. As I was picking out his casket, I was still expecting him to call and say that he would be home soon, or that he'd come and pick me up wherever I was. The call never came, of course. The warning signs to change my life were loud, but I was so self-absorbed in my own pain and despair that I completely ignored them. Instead, I let myself suffer through my grief. I didn't want to live anymore.

I never went back to the house that we had lived in together. Instead, I had movers pack our stuff and bring it to Jacksonville, where I was still staying with my parents. I couldn't bring myself to go back to the house. I couldn't stand seeing Jerry in my memory in every single room of that place but not seeing him there, real and solid, in front of me. There was too much pain in that place. I kept his photos all over the house in Jacksonville, though, like it used to be when he was alive. It made it feel normal, like maybe he was out of town and would be coming home any day. It helped me to see his face when I walked into a room.

After Jerry died, someone else took over the McDonald's thing, and I didn't talk to Uncle Jerry anymore. I don't think I even noticed, honestly; I was too distraught over losing my husband so suddenly and so painfully and wasn't thinking about Uncle Jerry at all. I took Jerry's death really badly, because I was driving, so I felt like I might as well have taken a gun and shot him in the head, since he had died as a direct result of what I had done, even though logically I knew that I hadn't done anything that anyone else wouldn't have done when I pulled out from the yield sign that day. Even still, I felt like it was all my fault. I had survivor's guilt. I had driver's guilt. I had such gut-wrenching guilt over my son losing his dad and the Colombos losing their beloved son. I often felt as though the wrong person had died; I should have died instead. I felt that if I could go back and redo it, I would, and my death would be the result, instead of Jerry's. Jerry was the provider, after all; Jerry had more people who loved him. He had so many more people who counted on him and needed him than I did.

Even though the Colombos didn't blame me—they had actually directly told me that if they hadn't been absolutely positive that it was an accident, I wouldn't have still been alive—I felt so terrible. My family had never been a loving, hugging, "it's going to be alright" kind of family, so I didn't feel as though I had a single person to turn to with my overwhelming grief. I just felt alone, even though I had my son there with me. But to be honest, I didn't even feel like Frankie could help me through the hell I was going through at the time. Being a mom was difficult and time-consuming, and it was not letting me grieve like I wanted to, properly and in a way in which I felt I could look back on Jerry and I together and remember it every second of the day. I had to keep doing mom things, even though I was still injured, even though my heart was shattered in my chest, even though I had no idea what to do without Jerry. Frankie would ask me where his daddy was, and I told him that his daddy was in a better place. I didn't know what else to say or any other way to make him understand that his daddy wasn't coming back. He would always ask why I was crying, and I couldn't keep telling him, "Because I miss your daddy so much." I was trying not to grieve out loud and in front of him, so that he wouldn't grieve. He was only three at the time, so I couldn't really have an in-depth conversation with him about what had happened. He had been used to Jerry being gone a lot, because he was on the road so often, so I suppose that at that time, he probably just thought his daddy was traveling on business like he usually did. I told him that he'd see Jerry again someday, although I don't think he understood what I was saying to him. I had to be careful not to cry when he might see me, because if I cried, Frankie would ask if it was better where daddy had gone, why was I crying. I'd tell him that I still had tears left in me for his daddy, and that it might take me a while to cry them all out.

I still cry about missing Jerry. People don't always understand it when I do. So many people out there think that twenty years of tears should be enough to stop crying. But our time was cut short. My parents got fifty years together – Jerry and I had nowhere near that. I was distraught because I had felt as though Jerry and I had just been getting ready to begin a different chapter in our lives, a better life, a better marriage. We had already fought about and worked through all of our issues. We had been in such a good place recently. I was excited for us to begin a new life together, that when the possibility of that life was taken away, I was really devastated. I didn't know what in the world I was going to do with my life and my son. I wasn't just grieving the life that Jerry had led, or the life we had led together, I was grieving the life that we never would lead, not now, not ever again. It's so hard, you know, to know that life could have gone such a completely different way. What if I had pulled away from the yield sign more slowly? What if I had waited altogether? What if we hadn't been on the road at all that day? It's hard to grieve for the past, the present, and the future. It felt like that's what I was doing anyway, even if I wasn't sure if I had the room in my heart to hold all of that. All I could think about, most of the time, was what things had been like for us. How we had been inseparable when we first started dating, how we laughed together all the time, about the time when we got a dog, a million little memories from when Frankie was a baby. The bad flashbacks didn't start coming until later. I had put him back up on a pedestal, because in my sorrow, I needed something to hold onto.

Before the funeral, there was a lot of strife in my house with me accusing my mother and father of not ever liking Jerry. There was a lot of yelling going on, so much so that my three-year-old son told my father to "quit yelling at Mommy!" Well, we packed up and left the house. We found a hotel suite until after the funeral, and, then, I looked for an apartment.

Jerry's Funeral

I've attended funerals in the past, but nothing could prepare me for this funeral. Jerry and I had discussed previously about our desires for our funeral arrangements, the type of music and flowers, etc. Jerry wanted a recording of the song, "My Way", sung by Frank Sinatra at a Catholic church. I spoke to the priest about this, and he said that since a choir would be singing, it wouldn't be appropriate for them to sing that song. However, he did ask the organ player to play it, and she did. When she did, both Mrs. Colombo and I lost it, crying uncontrollably. Once again, my heart was being ripped out of its socket. My chest felt like it was closing in on me and I couldn't breathe.

On my way outside, a good friend of mine hugged me and said that we've got it all wrong down here on earth. We are supposed to cry when someone is born into this old world and rejoice when they've passed on. Well, I was in no mood to rejoice, as I didn't even know for sure if I would ever see Jerry again. The whole concept of floating around in spirit form didn't sit well with me, as I thought that was what heaven was all about. Now, I know why it's so important to accept Jesus as your Savior and get to know Him personally. Unfortunately, I didn't have that relationship with Him, nor was I seeking it.

At the gravesite, I happened to look over my shoulder and see a line of men I didn't recognize, but it didn't matter. What mattered was that I wanted to be with my husband.

After the services, my father-in-law said to me, "Robin, no matter what, we're still family." Then, he told me he made some phone calls to warn anyone who wanted to get in touch with me or his grandson to forget it. I immediately thought to myself, *Hmmm! It's not the others I'm worried about knocking me off; it's him I'm concerned about!* That thought quickly faded. My father-in-law has always been the perfect gentleman. He doesn't talk just to be talking, but only speaks when necessary.

My heart was also breaking for my mother-in-law. I wanted to share my son with her to ease her pain, and I did. The guilt I was feeling about my husband's death was tremendous. I kept thinking it should have been me who died, instead of Jerry. After all, Jerry had been a good provider in his own way and loved his family.

As I saw my husband's body in the casket, I went through moments of denial. I was a desperate woman and would do anything to have had more time with Jerry. I thought of all the useless arguing, the hurtful words I could never take back. I sure know how damaging words can be and the great pain of knowing nothing can be done about it, once a person is dead.

After the funeral, I let Frankie stay with the Colombos in New

Smyrna Beach, Florida, for two reasons. He would have his own room and a nice place to play. Secondly, he would help Ma and Pa Colombo in their time of grieving, as he was their first grandchild. I would let sixteen-year-old Jennifer go off with her friends, while I continued to cry and cry. It was not just for my loss that I grieved, but for Jennifer's and Frankie's loss, too. The relief I sought did not come. If I had not had my children with me, it would have been so much worse. For their sake, safeguarding my sanity kept me going.

I can remember being in the mall and hearing children yelling for their daddy and my heart would break, knowing that Frankie wouldn't be calling out for his daddy. I kept telling myself to be strong and to not lose it. I had to remain strong for Frankie's sake. It was even hard when Curtis, Jennifer's father, would come around to pick her up. It just didn't seem fair for Frankie.

A friend of mine gave me a business card of a medium, so that I could contact Jerry on the other side. I made an appointment with this psychic and so-called medium. Being in such darkness and despair, I really believed what I was doing would be okay. Not once did it enter my mind that what I was doing had been the wrong decision. After the sessions, I really can't say it brought me much comfort; the comfort was short-lived. I just grasped at anything to feel Jerry's presence.

I remember, one day, I fell on the ground and screamed out in such agony, "Please, God, show me this isn't all there is!" I desperately needed proof that I would see my husband again. This just couldn't be all there was to this life.

About a month or so later, I started seeing my husband's spirit. I couldn't believe it at first, as I was trying to justify the things I was seeing by thinking I was just grief-stricken; that I was making myself see him. But he wouldn't go away. I would rub my eyes in disbelief and open them, and find out he was still there. Finally, I started looking forward to his visits. They brought me instant comfort, and I was so dependent upon them. I was actually able to read his lips and know what he was saying. A lifelong buddy of mine even caught me talking with Jerry. I politely asked him, "Do you mind? I'd like to be with my husband!" I didn't understand why so many people wanted to reason away these sightings and visions, as they were, indeed, real! Later, I would find out how I was opening myself to the devil's playground.

Therefore, evil shall come upon you; You shall not know from where it arises. And trouble shall fall upon you; You will not be able to put it off. And desolation shall come upon you suddenly, which you shall not know. Stand now with your enchantments and the multitude of your sorceries, in which you have labored from your youth. Perhaps you will be able to profit. Perhaps you will prevail.

Isaiah 47:11-12

If anyone loses a loved one, take heed to what I'm saying: you may at first receive comfort from a fortune teller, but at that time, you become a target for Satan's demons!

At the risk of going to prison for fraud, I engaged in illegal activities in order to keep up a certain lifestyle for myself and my kids. I wanted the nice cars, homes, and beautiful clothes for myself. All the toys and fine schools, I wanted for my kids. All of this without having to work a nine-tofive job. Once I had tasted the so-called "good life" of having everything I wanted without having to work for it, I wanted to do as little as possible, workwise, to maintain my lifestyle. Forgery and insurance and credit card fraud seemed pretty innocent and enabled me to live the way I had become accustomed to, while married to Jerry. It was not like robbing a bank or killing someone.

Surely, you did not hear. Surely, you did not know; Surely, from long ago, your ear was not opened. For I knew that you would deal very treacherously, and were called a transgressor from the womb.

Isaiah 48:8

I needed to see Jerry and so needed to talk with him. I needed his strength and comfort. Oh, God! The pain was unbearable. Jerry was the one that kept our two families from fighting. It didn't matter that I was wrong or right, Jerry would stand behind me 100 percent. He appeared to be a magical walking sign to our families that said everything was gonna be okay, so, everyone just stay cool. And they did as a whole.

What would I do now? How would I support Frankie and myself? My mother-in-law—Ma Colombo—jokingly said, "Now, it's up to us, Bella Mafia." This meant the women were taking over.

I got the moving van at my townhouse, when detectives and police came to arrest me on charges of grand theft and insurance and credit card fraud. Eventually, I was sentenced to three-and-a-half years in the state prison. It had only been a year since my husband's death. Life for me was not sweet during those years.

The next thing I knew, I was calling my mother-in-law from jail, awaiting my sentence. I said to her, "The Bella Mafia went down." Facing three-and-a-half years in the state prison seemed like a lifetime to me. My *lifetime*, whether in or out of prison, was really no life at all, I figured. Things just had to get better. Or would they?

CHAPTER 8

LIFE BEHIND BARS

When I got to Lowell State Prison, I lay back on my steel bunk. It was finally quiet with the lights out and everyone asleep. Everyone except me. Sleep eluded me. I looked around at my surroundings and couldn't believe I was going to be living there for three-and-a-half years! There were so many roaches that you would have to stuff paper in your ears, so they wouldn't crawl in there. Of course, there was no air conditioning. You slept so close to your neighbor that you could reach out and touch her. It gave a whole new meaning to the phrase, "Reach out and touch someone!" Having frail nerves, it didn't take much to send me into an emotional mess.

I remember being screamed at by an arrogant correctional officer over a frivolous matter. I ran all the way back to my cell, completely shaken up. When I got there, I ran straight to my bed, kneeled on the floor, grabbed my radio, and started screaming in it to God, "Take me, take me now. I can't stand it anymore. It hurts too damn bad!" I yelled, "Take my kids, take my family, take all my possessions, I don't care! I'm just too tired to fight."

Their hearts cried out to the Lord, O wall of the daughter of Zion. Let tears run down like a river day and night; Give yourself no relief; Give your eyes no rest.

Arise, cry out in the night, at the beginning of the watches. Pour out your heart like water before the face of the Lord. Lift your hands toward Him for the life of our young children, who faint from hunger at the head of every street.

Lamentations 2:18-19

I was so broken, and I felt totally helpless. While serving my state time, I toyed around with going to church. I met some wonderful volunteers, Barbara and Wanda. They prophesied over me, and one of them said God had bottled up my tears. She sensed a good spirit in me. This made me really cry, as I felt some hope for myself.

Later, in a meeting of 80 women, Wanda picked me out and said the Lord was going to break some strongholds in my life and my plans would fail, because He had other plans for me. Now, I'm thinking, I won't be going on work release. I was also afraid she would touch my head and expect me to fall back on the floor. I just felt uncomfortable with this myself—the unknown. I sure wanted to be in control. A great thought for one in prison!

At one of the services, I accepted Jesus as my Savior in Lowell State Prison, but that was the extent of it. Hey! I did this twenty-three years ago at summer camp, and nothing really changed in my life. I had no idea you could have a personal relationship with God and be serious with Him. It all seemed like a fairytale to me.

A short time later, I heard horror stories of a lot of strife going on in my mother-in-law's house. I know my son, Frankie, was suffering.

I was in a panic and didn't know what to do. When my mother-in-law brought Frankie to visit me, he asked me why I was sending his grandmother bad letters.

I was shocked and looked at her, then at him, and told him, "It's definitely not true."

Then Ma Colombo replies to Frankie, "That's not true. She is!" Can you imagine what was going through the mind of my four-year-old?

Here I was, trying to live in this place and knew my mother-in-law was trying to turn my own son away from me. Must I lose everything? Everything? Even my own flesh and blood?

An officer, whom I had highly respected, agreed with me that I needed to get my son away from his grandparents' home. I then asked my parents if they would keep Frankie, and could make arrangements for them to pick him up. They agreed, and I was so pleased. For now, I knew my parents wouldn't alienate my son from me, and he would be able to play with his sister, Jennifer.

My parents picked Frankie up and took him into their home. Now, he would have a newly redecorated room, complete wardrobe and toys, and even a swimming pool in the backyard. It was only a short distance to his day school and a park. He would also have many kids to play with in the neighborhood.

Don't get me wrong, Ma Colombo loved Frankie dearly. After all, he was their first grandson and my late husband's only son. I was concerned about his emotional and mental state, not being able to play with friends or talk with his sister over the phone. With my son and daughter having different fathers, the Colombos just could not see them as really being brother and sister; therefore, they couldn't see the need for them to be together.

At that time, I was very happy about the situation with Frankie being at my parent's home. I would be able to see Frankie twice a month at the prison, and even the other women inmates were seeing a difference in him.

As soon as we felt comfortable that the Colombos would not try to take Frankie to Sicily or Switzerland, where they had relatives, we were open to their getting Frankie every other weekend. My own father stated that he had no problem with this arrangement with the Colombos regularly having Frankie. Even one of the Colombo sons could come by and play with him. The visits were now set up, and things were starting to work out.

Meanwhile, I was starting to attend church services regularly. I was slowly seeking the things of God, and I mean slowly. I met some very inspiring Christians in prison, and two of them really stood out to me. The first one I'll call Bobbie. She and I had some very similar losses by way of family and missed opportunities. Bobbie had an inner peace and a very loving heart. When I would have visits with the prison psychiatrist, I knew he couldn't really help, because he only treated the symptoms with pills. Yet, in contrast, when Bobbie prayed for me, I felt a genuine peace come over me.

One afternoon, I just couldn't stop crying—with buckets of tears flowing down my face—Bobbie put her hands on my shoulders and looked me straight in the eyes. She said to me, "Robin, honey, I see a very warm heart and a wonderful spirit inside of you. God wants you to know that He has bottled up your tears, that you are special, and that He loves you." Nobody had sincerely ever told me they loved me—let alone God. Not even my own mother. I cried all the more. Now, my heart had a little hope in it, and I was beginning to believe I would have a good future somehow.

The other woman who was special to me during that time was Sandra. Sandra would come regularly as a guest speaker in our chapel. Please understand, I was only a baby Christian, having just received Jesus into my heart and baptized. After one service, there were about 70 of us lined up to go back to our dorms when Sandra walked by us. She stopped, came back to me, and said, "I have a message for you." She had never before seen me and seemed to pick me out of the 70 women. I just kind of laughed it off to my friend.

However, another week rolls around and my friend and I went to hear the message for me. We sat in the back, not wanting to be called up front for prayer or fall down like some women after they were prayed for. The sermon related to some issues that I was dealing with the previous week. I thought that this would be the message for me. As we were making our way out of the chapel, before Sandra started to pray for people, she suddenly called out, "Where is Robin?" Many women pointed to me. I had never told her my name.

Under my breath I was saying, "Please, don't let this woman embarrass me!" I went up front. She looked at me and put her hand on my shoulder, and began to prophesy. At the moment, I thought she was some kind of psychic, yet now, I look back and know this was true prophecy.

She stated, "The Lord wants me to tell you He will be releasing a lot of strongholds over you and whatever your plans are, they will not happen. He has other plans for you. You will be ministering to others." When Sandra prophesied to me, I only had a week before going into work release.

I thought, *Oh, no, I'm not going into work release, go home, and put all things behind me and begin a new life. Surely, Sandra had me confused with someone else, and what do I know about ministering?* When I brought up all these things to my dormmate, Bobbie, she just patted me on the back and said not to worry, and that I would be learning.

Sure enough, after two-and-a-half years, I was saying goodbye to the hot, roach-infested dorms, and because of my physical freedom, I forgot the prophetic words of my being set free and ministering to others. In hindsight, I think it seems amazing how little human beings give thought to the spiritual areas of their lives. Yet, I was to find out in the near future just how much the spiritual affects the mental, emotional, and physical areas of a person's life.

Work Release

The plan was for me to be in prison work for six months and then be allowed to get my own job. In July 2001, I began digging ditches in the Florida sun. Some days, the roaches back at Lowell didn't seem so bad after all. After three weeks, some of the ladies ran back and told me that the major wanted to see me. I was not concerned, because I hadn't done anything wrong.

The major took me where the business offices were located and into a room where two tall, well-dressed men were also waiting. My height is five-feet-one-inch, and they were at least six-feet-four-inches. When I looked up at them, they immediately flashed two FBI badges at me. They pulled out a colorful poster and spread it out before me. I saw a Monopoly game in bold letters and a bunch of photos on top, with me being one of them. I felt a rush of nerves threatening to choke me. Above my name were bold letters and the word *incarcerated*. Above my husband's name was *deceased*. Uncle Jerry was right in the center of the poster, positioned so as to be the head of the whole scam.

The agents asked me to tell them all I knew. I said my two children were out there and I was concerned about their safety, so they should leave me their numbers and I would get back with them. When they left, I was told the major wanted to see me. He told me that I was being shackled and sent back to prison and placed in confinement. Immediately, tears sprang into my eyes, as I had never been in cell confinement—only in lock-in dorms. My first thoughts were that this was because I had not talked to the feds. So, I told the major that I wanted to talk with them. He told me it was too late. As the agents walked past a glass window, I yelled at them and told them I would talk. I hadn't done anything, yet because there was an ongoing investigation, I could be headed back to prison.

The agents escorted me back into the conference room. One agent informed me that there were federal agents across the U.S. questioning the participants at that very moment. The agents started asking me questions, and I just nodded my head either "yes" or "no". They were very polite and even asked me if I wanted something to eat. I refused their offer, as my stomach was tied up in knots.

They asked if there was a TV we could watch, so the major and another officer took us into the TV room. The major closed off that area for us, and we turned on the six o'clock news. The Attorney General, John Ashcroft, was speaking to many reporters and the country, telling them about the McDonald's Monopoly Game fraud. He was quick to exonerate the McDonald's Corporation of any foul play. Then, I saw Uncle Jerry in handcuffs, being escorted by U.S.

Marshals. Immediately, my heart sank, and my legs felt like Jell-O. I needed a cigarette break really bad!

I told the agents that my deceased husband had been the number two guy, and Uncle Jerry was the number one man in the scam. I related to them how Jerry and I had been so thrilled at the time of being able to give one of our family members the winning ticket. The winner just happened to be my father!

Well, here I was about ready to break free of my old lifestyle when it came back to haunt me. It was getting close to my birthday, and here I was going back to confinement. What a present! I was placed in a tour-type bus with all the other inmates, except I was the only female. Only, this was no tour, with handcuffs and leg chains on us, as a good reminder. We were being taken to the federal facility in Jacksonville, Florida. When I got out of the bus, the U.S. Marshal said I was going someplace else—McClenny—a place where I would be safer and better taken care of than before. The new facility I arrived at was located in Baker County, Florida, a much smaller place than where I thought I was going. When I got there, I couldn't believe it. It was almost like *The Andy Griffith Show*, the old TV series. The nurse was even called Aunt B. Everyone really seemed concerned about our care. When they saw I was having a hard time coping with what I foresaw as a 40-year sentence, my anxiety level was beyond control. They placed me back on Zoloft for depression. And a new medication, called Xanax, for anxiety.

In "Mayberry", another inmate began telling me how to contact the dead. I was getting pretty excited over this, as I pondered the counsel of my late husband and wondered what he would tell me to do and what was going to happen. We started contacting many people's loved ones on the other side on a daily basis. We so wanted their advice, but what we received was uncertain and very general information.

Your prophets have seen for you false and deceptive visions; They have not uncovered your iniquity, to bring back your captives, but have envisioned for you false prophecies and delusions.

Lamentations 2: 14

Soon, the battle was on between my family and Jerry's. It seemed only my family was indicted for the mail fraud of the McDonald's Monopoly scheme, not Jerry's family. They weren't even questioned. I was charged with conspiracy, even though I didn't actually do anything. Bitterness pervaded my soul, as I was taking the fall, when others should have gone with me. I told my family not to let Frankie around my husband's family.

The Colombo family hired an attorney with the hope of getting custody of my son. After being informed that they needed grounds, they called up the H.R.S. and told them that my family abused Frankie. This was quickly proven to be a lie. They used the fact that my father, one of the fraudulent winners of the Monopoly game was indicted, and my mother had health problems, to attempt to justify the accusations. Even though my father never went to prison for the crime, he paid everything back and then some. My father had served his country faithfully in the military and had no previous criminal record. Still, Frankie was awarded to my ex-husband's family. My father was never allowed to testify in court. High-priced attorneys can make a difference. I never thought for one moment that my parents would lose custody.

When I found out about the custody news, I collapsed in my cell. I then heard the echoes of people's voices saying, "Breathe, Colombo, breathe!"

This can't be happening, I thought.

Is it nothing to you, all you who pass by? Behold and see if there is any sorrow like my sorrow, which has been brought on me, which the Lord has inflicted in the day of His fierce anger.

For these things I weep; My eye, my eye overflows with water; Because the comforter, who should restore my life, is far from me. My children are desolate, because the enemy prevailed.

Lamentations 1: 12, 16

Two women sergeants ran to pick me up and carry me to the medical facility. Nothing but anguish gripped my heart. I felt as though I was in a tunnel as the nurses gave me shots to calm me. Again, I heard voices that sounded like echoes in the far away distance. I faded away into semi-unconsciousness. One of the sergeants was holding me on the floor, rocking me back-and-forth, trying to comfort me. I felt our hearts connect in a pure way as she was suffering with me. Yet, I was not to be comforted. I was taken back to my cell, but they didn't leave me alone. The nurses and sergeants were talking, discussing how they could give me comfort. All to no avail.

I screamed out to my late husband, "Jerry, please! Help me! Your family has taken our son, and I can't hang on anymore." My voice became a hollow echo as I cried out. There was no response from anyone. No comfort. Nothing. All who were in my cell left, as the medication began to put me to sleep.

When I awoke, an officer told me that my son and daughter had been granted a special visit with me. My fellow inmates helped me to get dressed. I had to be strong for my kids, as I couldn't let them see me fall apart. I stepped into the room where they were waiting. Running straight to my little boy, I told them no matter what happened, I loved them with all my heart. My son's little lips quivered with grief, and as I looked to my daughter, she, too, was stricken with heartache. They suffered at such young ages, all because of me. As I was returned to my cell, all I wanted to do was rid myself of this deep emotional pain and anguish. I butt my head against the wall of my cell, hoping the physical pain would somehow override it.

All your enemies have opened their mouth against you. They hiss and gnash their teeth. They say, "We have swallowed her up! Surely this is the day we have waited for; We have found it! We have seen it!"

The Lord has done what He purposed; He has fulfilled His word which He commanded in days of old. He has thrown down and has not pitied, and He has caused an enemy to rejoice over you. He has exalted the horn of your adversaries.

Their hearts cried out to the Lord, " O wall of the daughter of Zion! Let tears run down like a river day and night, give yourself no relief; Give your eyes no rest."

Arise, cry out in the night, at the beginning of the watches. Pour out your heart like water before the face of the Lord. Lift your hands toward Him, for the life of your young children, who faint from hunger at the head of every street.

Lamentations 2:16-19

After the hearing pre-trial for the McDonald's Monopoly scam, I was finally released on the work release program and living with my parents. Having lost my husband, custody of my son, spending three-and-a-half years in prison, and facing another 40-year term, I was just going through the bare motions of living day by day. I accepted Jesus as my Savior, but didn't have enough of a relationship with Him to call out to Him. I forgot the God who saved me! (Psalms 106:21) I was putting God on the same level as my late husband, calling out to both of them for help. I never, ever thought I'd be a widow or lose my children, and nearly lose my mind, too.

But these two things shall come to you in a moment, in one day. They shall come upon you in their fullness because of the multitude of your sorceries, for the great abundance of your enchantments.

For you have trusted in your wickedness; You have said, 'No one sees me'; Your wisdom and your knowledge have warped you; And you have said in your heart, I am, and there is no one else besides me.

Therefore, evil shall come upon you; You shall not know from where it arises. And trouble shall fall upon you; You will not be able to put it off. And desolation shall come upon you suddenly, which you shall not know.

Stand now with your enchantments, and the multitude of your sorceries, in which you have labored from your youth— perhaps you will be able to profit, perhaps you will prevail.

You are wearied in the multitude of your counsels; Let now the astrologers, the stargazers, and the monthly prognosticators stand up and save you from what shall come upon you.

Isaiah 47:9-13

Not ever having read the Bible before, I didn't have a clue as to what was written in the Old Testament. So much of what I was going through was already written in Isaiah. All the counsel I received and medication from doctors and so-called counsel from mediums were worthless. I had not turned to the main source of life for any and all counsel, for I did not know Him. I could clearly see that meeting God through accepting Jesus was one thing, but really turning my life over to Him and knowing Him was another thing. It was sad that I didn't even know the Lord enough to realize it was He who could really help me get through all this.

My next action, I thought, was my only option—ending my life with pills. Taking about 100 pills with my coffee would end it all, and I would be with Jerry. No more pain; no more anguish. As I drank my coffee with an overdose, I looked up to heaven and said, "Jerry, here I come." Three hours later, my eyes popped open. I wasn't even sleepy! I had just swallowed 60 pills for anxiety and 30 tablets for pain! And I was wide awake! What the!

Really angry at myself, I jumped up and ran downstairs in my parents' home. I ran into the kitchen seeking a knife, since there were no guns in the house. No one was around, as it was about three o'clock in the morning. I got a paring knife, ran back upstairs to get a towel, and ran to my room to end this madness in my life. I sat in front of my free-standing mirror yoga style, picked up the knife, took a deep breath and stabbed the knife deep inside my neck.

I couldn't believe it! No blood was shooting out. *Maybe I should have gone deeper,* I thought. So, I began to probe deeper, searching for an artery. Finally, I saw some blood, so I withdrew the knife, wiped it off and decided to go ahead and sleep, thinking I had little chance of ever waking up. Before I closed my eyes, my last thoughts were again on Jerry. So, I told him once again that I would be with him soon. I drifted off to sleep.

As daylight came through the window, I opened my eyes only to find myself wide-awake. I just could not believe this! I had taken all those pills and used a knife on one of the most vulnerable parts of my body, yet I was still alive. In fact, very much alive!

The same voice I had heard earlier, telling me that I was worthless, without any hope, and that everyone would be better off without me, was once again echoing those same thoughts through my head. I was not really connected to Jesus all that much, so I was an easy prey for Satan's lies and schemes. Even so, God won that battle and Satan lost. Little did I know that the enemy of my soul would fight all the harder to get me once again.

Next, I went downstairs as if nothing had happened to me, not even aware that the side of my neck was mutilated and parts of it were inside out. My mother passed me by and asked, "What in the world happened?"

I casually said, "Oh, I sliced my throat." I was still pretty numb from all the pills, and this just added to my sense of failure in all areas of my life. After several days of mostly sleeping, my body started tightening up. My friend called and told me that my body was going through massive withdrawals. She told my father what was happening, and I wanted to go to the hospital emergency room. When I arrived, they took my vital signs and rushed me back to the

ICU. A little later, the doctor noticed my neck and asked me what had happened. I told him and he asked me why I had attempted to commit suicide.

After some brief explanations, the doctor patted my arm and said, "Mrs. Colombo, everything is going to be fine." When my cubicle curtains were pulled back, I was staring at two security guards.

One of the guards leaned over me and asked, "Mrs. Colombo, what is it like being a mafia wife?" I told him to take a good look at me, and no further explanations were needed. Since I had tried to take my own life, it got me an all-expenses-paid stay at the nut-hut or county psychiatric ward.

When I arrived at the high-risk area of the psych unit, I didn't get much rest, as the doctors were examining my throat to see what damage I had done. It was too late to stitch up my neck, so they just patched it up and let me sleep. I didn't get much sleep though, as my body was in a state of detoxification. I was feeling awful. A psychiatrist came by to visit and make sure I wouldn't try suicide again. I told her that I might as well stick around, since the pills and the knife didn't do me in. She ordered me a small dose of drugs for my anxiety.

Once I arrived back home, my thoughts turned to my son, whom I had missed very much. My in-laws had changed their phone number, and now, I couldn't even hear his voice. I found my brother-in-law's phone number and left some nasty messages, threatening them all with the feds. I started talking with reporters and anyone who would listen. My attorney called me and asked what in the world I was doing. I told him I was talking with reporters, and he said I wasn't allowed to do that. So, I asked him to set up a meeting with the FBI, because I was bringing down the Colombo family along with me. The very next day, my attorney set up a meeting with my prosecutor and an FBI agent. We arrived at the federal building in Jacksonville and went into a conference room, where the four of us sat down to talk. Suddenly, I realized that this didn't feel like a friendly meeting. Sure enough, I wasn't expecting what happened next. The prosecutor stared me straight in the eyes and said, "Mrs. Colombo, you have threatened the Colombo family."

"Yes," I said, "but not with violence! I threatened them with you!" They didn't want to hear anything I had to say, and said that if I tried to contact that family, I would be right back in jail. Then, they both stood and left the room.

I couldn't believe what I had just heard. When what had just happened sunk in, I jumped out of my seat and chased after the two men. They were a good way down the hall when I leaned up against the wall and yelled, "No. Stop! You can't do this. They have my son." I collapsed. My attorney was lifting me up as anguish once again gripped my heart.

For these things I weep; My eye, my eye overflows with water; Because the comforter, who should restore my life, is far from me. My children are desolate because the enemy prevailed. Let all their wickedness come before You, and do to them as You have done to me. For all my transgressions; For my sighs are many, and my heart is faint.

Lamentations 1:16, 22

In a mindless stupor, I returned home to my bed, not being able to really think about anything. I just stared at the walls of the house. There was no TV or radio on; no sound whatsoever. I remember lying there and thinking to myself, *this is how people lose their minds.* I even had a mental vision of me sitting in an insane asylum, and it was a very bleak picture. I was sitting in a rocking chair with a blanket covering my legs. In this vision, my son is a grown man; I can see him asking the nurses if I can hear him. I do, in fact, hear him, but cannot speak; I just rock back-and-forth. That was exactly how I saw my future.

On September 16, 2002, I was to be sentenced for the McDonald's Monopoly scam. The prosecutor dropped all mail fraud charges, but one. Because I already had a criminal record, I was informed that I would be sent back to federal prison to serve my time.

The McDonald's case was so large that the sentencing had to be broken up into many sessions. In my group, I was the second person called up. I walked up to the judge's bench, before a very packed courtroom, and I could feel every eye on me. The judge handed me down an 18-month sentence, with three years of probation. My heart sank, and I couldn't wait to get out of there fast enough. They also gave me an astronomical restitution fine of $2 million. They knew I didn't receive any money from the scam, but they added up the monies the fraudulent winners received, and gave the restitution to me, a poverty-stricken widow. I really wasn't even one of the winners. I was guilty of conspiracy in the case, by just knowing about it and not saying anything. I didn't want my father involved, but Jerry went behind my back and kept suggesting it to him. My father gave in. But, to give me such a fine was absurd! Here in the U.S., with one of the greatest judicial systems in the world, justice was not served.

I was now at a place of starting over with my life, even if it meant doing more time in prison. I had some hope—some, I say—that I would get through all of this. I sensed some big, black cloud following me wherever I went. Later, I seemed to be moving towards more hopelessness as the day approached for me to go to prison. Suicide was out. I had already failed miserably at that. I could only scream out to God to fix me or take me, one or the other. What purpose was I serving on this earth? Was I serving grief?

My mother and I were at each other's throats. We had so hurt each other through the years; we were just walking wounded, facing each other. How does one get rid of a wound when your mother tells you she wishes she never had you? I now know the arch-enemy of my soul, Satan, was behind all the chaos in my life, and he could only bother me as I opened my life to allow the entrance of sin. But, a person without a growing knowledge of God and His Word is really oblivious to the schemes of the devil.

But the natural man does not receive the things of the Spirit of God, for they are foolishness to him; nor can he know them, because they are spiritually discerned.

I Corinthians 2:14

On October 25th, I was sent to federal prison in Tallahassee, Florida. Oh, how I missed hearing the voice of my son, as it had been almost two years since I had heard it. After six months in Tallahassee, I was taken to Coleman Camp and worked there in landscaping. After that, I was taken to a halfway house in Ocala, Florida, where I worked as a waitress.

Then, the day came when my father and mother brought me Frankie. He and I couldn't get enough of each other. He said it was the best day of his life. And mine, too. My heart swelled with joy!

When I was released from prison in December of 2003, I couldn't stop grieving for my deceased husband. I was out on probation, but could still sense a black cloud following me. The thoughts kept nagging me that I wouldn't be able to take care of my son. These thoughts led to depressed feelings, which led to some very rash actions.

My girlfriend and I had always kidded each other that some day we would fall for some "old guy", and he would take care of us. Well, those seeds of thought came back to me at this time and produced a harvest. Sure enough, I fell for, but was not in love with, a much older guy with the very idea of being taken care of by him.

My grand scheme was when I got Frankie back, we would have it made with this old guy. He wasn't even an old gentleman, but downright malicious and evil, as I would find out soon enough. It got to where I didn't even want to be sober around him. Things came to a halt when I crashed his Explorer SUV into a concrete wall and totaled it out at $20,000 worth of damage. I broke my leg and was laid up for several months. More inside and outside pain, so more pills. When those failed, I tried drinking and cocaine.

When I went to see my probation officer in Ocala—who was a really good man—I felt like I could share anything with him. One day while visiting him, I just started crying uncontrollably and finally cried out to him, "I just want to be happy." At the time, I knew nothing of the Scriptures.

Why do you cry about your affliction? Your sorrow is incurable. Because of the multitude of your iniquities. Because your sins have increased, I have done these things to you.

Jeremiah 30:15

With understanding, I can see how I was being corrected by a loving, heavenly Father, but also one of justice. Out of the kindness of his heart, my probation officer transferred me back to Jacksonville. Moving back in with my parents, I immediately went to work in a beauty salon.

I was still under a doctor's care for my anxiety, back problems, and damaged leg from the recent automobile accident.

What I had hoped to be a turning point in my life was not to be. Working steadily over a short period of time, I was able to buy some jewelry, nice clothing, and by this time, was driving another vehicle. However, they all lost their attraction very quickly.

I was seeing a psychologist and would usually end up sobbing endlessly in her office. I remember saying to her one time, "I hope to find my purpose in life before I am 80!" What a silly statement, for what could I accomplish at the age of 80? I told her that I felt like I was just taking up space on this earth. Even my co-workers, my fellow hairstylists, could sense I was just going through the motions.

Around August of 2004, my daughter's grandfather died. At the funeral, my first love, Curtis Ethridge, and I were reunited after many years. He was very distraught, of course, at his father's passing. We decided I would drive him home and stay at his house in Baldwin, Florida. I enjoyed spending time with him and getting reacquainted. I even thought about developing a new relationship with him. Later, I read from Hosea 2:7 about going and returning to my first lover or husband. Wow, what another parallel from the scriptures to my life. Instead, I made alcohol and drugs my companions. At least they did not fight and argue, and didn't hurt me like another human being would. What a lie I believed.

In December of 2004, it was time for me to be sentenced for a former violation of probation charge. My daughter and I pleaded my case before the judge. U.S. Marshals were ready to escort me back to prison, but I was given a reprieve until January 2005—due to the holidays—and was then sent to a halfway house in Jacksonville. I was so excited, because this would be the first Christmas I had spent with my family in five years. Yet, with all this favor and my outside circumstances seeming to come together, I was still fighting some kind of darkness inside of me. Quickly, I reverted to alcohol and drugs to lessen the pressure and the pain. Others would pass off my problems as being bipolar and some psychological jargon, which gave me no understanding whatsoever.

No one would listen when I told them I was battling demonic spirits. Voices mixed with strong feelings of self-hate, rejection, and suicide would invade my very soul. It was beyond some very intelligent people's comprehension, such as the psychologists and psychiatrists. These professionals were dealing only with mental matters, and addressed nothing of the heart and spiritual matters. They just could not and would not see it. My psychologist was trying to reprogram my behavior, but she wasn't reaching the root cause of my actions, a wounded and broken heart, filled with the many scars of sin.

As I entered the halfway house in January of 2005, I wanted to work seven days a week as a hairstylist. I would work seven days just to keep busy, but six days was the limit. Several weeks after I entered into the halfway house, I got a call from my daughter saying her father was in the hospital, and things didn't look good for him. He had cirrhosis of the liver. It would be only a few hours before Curtis would pass on. I couldn't believe what I was hearing. I hung up and ran screaming, "No, not again!" The two loves of my life now gone, Jerry and Curtis, and both of my children left fatherless. What next?

I was granted time with my daughter and Curtis. At his bedside, I thanked him for a beautiful daughter, and we told each other that we would always love each other. I turned away, seeing Curtis alive for the last time, and then cried in my girlfriend's arms.

Curtis's mother, the one I had called a Jesus freak many years ago, was a praying woman, and before Curtis died, he had received Jesus into his heart as Savior. This was some consolation for me.

I returned to the halfway center and turned to pain pills and not to God to relieve my suffering. It seemed a party was going on in the rooms with it being Super Bowl Sunday, in Jacksonville, no less. Everybody partied too much, and in no time at all, we were thrown out of the halfway center! Back to my parents' house I went. When I got there, I just lay in my bed crying and crying. I thought about both of my husbands dying, their children being left fatherless, and suddenly it hit me. Both Jerry and Curtis died on each other's birthday. Curtis died on February 7, which was Jerry's birthday, and Jerry died on the 22nd of May, Curtis's birthday.

What did all this mean, I asked myself? At the time, I began to relive in my mind different events of my life. My life had been so bleak, serving no real purpose. Why couldn't I just go home to God? I cried. Anguish was, once again, ripping through my body. Every ounce of my being seemed distraught. I desperately needed help! Someone. Just someone to comfort me. I didn't know how to comfort Jennifer on the loss of her father, as I felt her pain as well as my own.

Neither she, nor I, had ever read the Bible. She started reading it the night of her father's death. I was unable to give her any input, because I had none. I just crawled into bed with her, so she wouldn't be alone. My heart was breaking again as I fell asleep.

A few weeks later on a Friday, I entered the hair salon where I worked, and there were no clients waiting. It was strange, as Fridays and Saturdays were our busiest days. The only people in the salon were my boss, Penny, a couple of co-workers, and another couple. Penny introduced me to the couple—Ed and Sherry—who were Christians, and had been getting their haircut there, as well as fellowshipping with Penny on Sundays. At that time, Penny asked them if they would pray for us. We all held hands in a circle, and in a moment, Sherry started prophesying over me. I had heard this before in the state prison when Sandra prophesied a message over me there. Sherry spoke to me and said the Lord said I was straddling the fence with Him. I immediately thought, *that's right*, and the words jolted me. So that night—I will never forget—we decided to have a Bible study in the salon after we closed for business. At that time, guys and girlfriends started asking me if I wanted to go out. I told them all the same thing. "No! I'm staying for the Bible study." This statement and decision were to change my life forever.

CHAPTER 9

TRUE SPIRITUAL JOURNEY BEGINS

At the Bible Study that night, everybody was invited to stay, but only Penny, myself, Ed and Sherry, and their ten-year-old adopted daughter were there. Ed and Sherry adopted her in Asia, where they often went to minister to the underground church. I felt so blessed to be able to learn from them. I hung on to every word. Ed was speaking, and, then, floods of tears started welling up in my eyes. I noticed all of them looking at me and Ed saying, "You are special. A fighter. There is a great purpose for you." Mind you, I wasn't feeling very special. There seemed to be so little fight left in me. I was feeling more like the Cowardly Lion in *The Wizard of Oz*. After I told them a brief summary of my life, and pouring my heart out to the group, we all held hands and prayed. I noticed while I was standing there, my legs started feeling like Jell-O. Quickly, my mind saw people falling down, and I didn't want to do that, so I sat in a salon chair. No one actually fell down, as I had seen before in prison, and I sure didn't want to. The next thing I knew, people were laying hands on me and praying in a strange language. I just closed my eyes and listened. I peeked a couple of times to see what was happening.

Now, everyone began to pray louder and louder, and more intensely. I closed my eyes and thought to myself, *I wonder why they pray like this?* I had heard about it, but never understood it.

When they finished praying, Sherry started rubbing my back and said to me, "Your season of grieving is over. The soul ties between you and your husband, and your mother-in-law have been broken." The meaning of this was that the mental and emotional bonds that kept me hurting were over. I never once said anything to her about anything I had gone through with them. Amazingly, God was speaking through her. She then asked her ten-year-old daughter if God had placed anything in her heart to share with us.

Her daughter said, "Yes. God says the reason we pray in tongues is so that the devil can't understand us." Wow! What an awesome time that night was.

I couldn't wait to tell my parents what had happened. They listened, but they thought it was more cute than real. My mother and father had a hard time believing anything that you couldn't see or touch. Going to church was an unspoken topic around our house.

Several weeks later, we wanted to have another Bible study, but Brother Ed was away in the Far East ministering to the native people there. So, his wife Sherry, along with her good friend, Sally, and my boss, Penny, got together at the salon. It was a Saturday night, and people who knew me couldn't believe I was willing to give up going out on a Saturday night for a Bible study.

But I had experienced something real and good and pure with these people before, and I was determined to find out as much as I could about God. I felt such an urging! I just did. I knew I had a return court date to answer for my being kicked out of the halfway house and breaking probation.

The friend who came with Sherry, Sally, asked me to tell her a little about myself. I did. She asked me if I had ever been involved in any form of witchcraft. I responded yes. Next, she asked me if I had some kind of charm to get rid of. I couldn't think of any at the time. I forgot about the object I used to call up the dead with! Later, when I did remember, I wasted no time finding it and getting rid of it.

Sally, now standing close to me, held my head. She told me to name all the demonic forces I had by first name, and I did. Sally asked me how I felt. I told her my chest was tight. She started praying in tongues while holding my head. We both ended up sitting on the floor, and Sally asked for the assistance of Penny and Sherry. The next thing I knew, I was freezing cold, and Penny was holding my legs down, because I seemed to have lost all control of them. They began to pray louder and louder. Penny yelled, "Get out of my friend!" They were having to hold me tighter and tighter. I was freaked out by this time, because whatever was in me didn't want to leave. Then, I started to feel embarrassed that my body was acting the way it was in front of these people. About 30 minutes later, everyone stopped praying, and they released me. Penny asked me how I was doing, and in a shocked voice, I told her I was fine. Sally told me they had just cast a Spirit of Jezebel out of me. They told me that this spirit was one that manipulated men to get what they wanted from them. My friend Penny said, "No, not Robin!" And I said, "Oh, yes. I've been that way all my life and really didn't realize it."

When I was at home now, all I wanted to do was watch TBN (Trinity Broadcasting Network). I wanted to hear and absorb all that I could about God. I would sit up for hours watching all these inspiring people of God. I still didn't pick up a Bible to read, for I was relying on others to feed me spiritually.

Not long after watching *The Passion of Christ*, and seeing Jesus being horribly beaten and then crucified, I never forgot how ashamed and unworthy I felt—and how holy and sinless He was. At this moment, the reality of the Lamb, slain from the foundation of the world for all of mankind, became so real to me. Many years before, forty to be exact, I had cried and said, "No, no!" when my baby lamb was slain on a tree in Greece. Yes, hanging from a tree! Even though I was delivered from demonic spirits and the dark cloud that hung over me most of my life, I knew God still had much work to do in me.

During that time, I had to report to my probation officer three times a week, and punctually at 8:30 a.m. I really didn't care about being punctual. Once again, I felt my life was just a shell, with very little life in it. I desperately needed to feel loved and wanted. In some ways, I felt my life was still cursed. Each time I drove to the federal building to report to my probation officer, I was not sure whether I would be free to leave or hauled off to prison.

Early one morning, when I pulled up to my parents' home with so much anguish bottled up inside me, I wrapped my arms around the steering wheel, laid my head on it, and then sobbed and sobbed and sobbed. Torment and pain were ripping through my soul. While hunched over the steering wheel, I felt lashes across my back. They weren't painful, but very real. It was as if I was being stricken with a whip, like Jesus was. At that moment, the Lord took over my thoughts. I started feeling Jesus' pain and sorrow and also that of my late husband. Believe me, this experience was so real. It was as if I was going into a new level of knowing God, and I didn't even know what was happening. I look back now and see how through the sessions at the hair salon, the Lord was dealing with me in my desperate condition. Hosea 2:2-5 was preparing me for things to come.

Bring charges against your mother, bring charges; For she is not My wife, nor am I her Husband! Let her put away her harlotries from her sight, and her adulteries from between her breasts; Lest I strip her naked and expose her, as in the day she was born, and make her like a wilderness, and set her like a dry land, and slay her with thirst. I will not have mercy on her children, for they are the children of harlotry. For their mother has played the harlot; She who conceived them has behaved shamefully for she said, 'I will go after my lovers, who give me my bread and my water, my wool and my linen, my oil and my drink.

In April of 2005, my good friend Penny and I went to the federal court for a hearing and a subsequent hearing one week later. This was for the charge of breaking parole when I was kicked out of the halfway house. We were very confident we would not be there for long, but this was not the case.

While Penny and I were seated in the courtroom, and my attorney was sitting behind us, I tried to ask him what was going to happen. He kept insisting we talk after court was dismissed. Little did he know that my level of intensity was rising more and more. Next thing, I'm seated at the defendant's table with my attorney. The prosecutor and probation officer were seated to my left. I just happened to look down and see my attorney's notes with the amount of time he was requesting that I serve. I lost it! I screamed out loud, "Oh God, they can't do this to me!" I ran past my attorney and right outside the courtroom doors. I utterly collapsed. I felt drained of all life.

Penny, who was also my boss at the salon, was standing over me.

She tried to comfort me and said to me, "Robin, try to pull yourself together. They are not going to take you away."

I wiped my tears and asked, "They're not?" I feebly composed myself and sat back down at the defendant's table. All of a sudden, five U.S. Marshals came towards me and removed my jewelry and belt. I said goodbye to my friend. I had no idea where they were taking me.

I was taken to a private holding cell in the building. After several hours, the U.S. Marshals took me out to a van to transport me to a small jail outside of Jacksonville, in Nassau County. I am very thankful that they didn't take me to the city jail, as it was a very rough and unsafe place to be.

I arrived with tears flowing down my cheeks. One of the U.S. Marshals told the nurse on duty that I was to be put on suicide watch. I repeatedly told them I had no intention of trying to harm myself. They didn't want to hear it. They told me I would have to stay on suicide watch until I saw a psychiatrist. It was Friday evening, so I knew I'd be in this cell until at least Monday morning. I had no clothes on as I entered the freezing cell. I put a little plastic mat underneath the metal slab bed and found the warmest spot available.

Now, I was under the metal slab completely. I was naked and freezing, with the vent blowing cold air on me. One may ask why they had cold air blowing in a suicide watch cell? I found out later that they did this to keep the inmate so concerned about keeping warm that thoughts of suicide were far from their mind. I refused any food, even water. The toilet didn't work, and I had been reduced down to nothing. I was surrounded by cold concrete and metal—nothing living, except myself, and barely at that. I sensed that this was as close to death as I could be. I was just subsisting with only a little hope.

"Now, therefore," says the LORD, "Turn to Me with all your heart, with fasting, with weeping, and with mourning."

Joel 2:12

This was exactly what I was doing...weeping, mourning, and fasting. As I lay there day after day, the officers and inmate trustees labeled me as crazy. I could hear them outside my cell, laughing and gawking at me as if I were a freak show. I didn't care. I didn't care about anything. My food was slid to me on the floor, but I wouldn't even look at it, much less eat it.

I was in a state of total despair, as I'd never been before. Finally, I screamed out to God, "Please, help me!" No one was there to comfort me.

After day five in the suicide cell, something was to happen that would forever change my life. I was still lying under the metal bed, not having seen a doctor yet. I wasn't even looking forward to speaking to a psychiatrist and rehashing all I'd been through. I sure was tired of my horrible past becoming my present and reaching forth and becoming my future. It was late afternoon. While I was crying out to God, I happened to drift off to sleep. As I slept, I became really warm, and I had an extremely bright vision in my dream.

In my dream, I was holding up my left hand, while another, larger hand was placing a ring with diamonds and sapphires on my ring finger. It was a divine vision, but I didn't have a clue as to what it meant. I realized later, that I was engaged to Christ and eventually would become part of His bride! The dream had such an impact on me that I just couldn't put it into words.

I was awakened by a loud noise. My cell opened, and a guard brought in a double extra-large green jumpsuit. I am a size five. He told me to put it on, as I was going to see the doctor. I was still feeling much apprehension. With many lined up to see the doctor, the officers told me that I would be first. I must have been a high priority.

I sat down with the doctor, and she asked me if I had been here before. I said no. She looked at my name and said, "Your name sounds familiar." I got the impression that she may have heard my name from one of the many news stations. Then, she asked me if I was the same Robin Colombo who was involved in the McDonald's Monopoly case? Of course, I knew she was referring to the story where my late husband's family had taken my son while I was in Baker County Jail.

I responded, "Yes. I'm one and the same." I must have looked pitiful to her in the oversized jumpsuit, and being dirty and smelly. She got up and hugged me. She was the one who counseled me in 2001, while I was in Baker County. She was now working in Jacksonville, Duval County, and would drive for about an hour when I had my nervous breakdown over Frankie's custody being given to my in-laws.

Now, I understood the hug. A hug of compassion came from this doctor who had followed my case through the different times of incarceration in various counties. I was beginning to see God's hand and heart in His care for me. I was experiencing real care and concern here.

Now, it was becoming clear to me. I had met this particular doctor before. She asked me questions to get caught up on what was happening in my life now. She told me that I had left a good impression on her from our first counseling session, and she never forgot me. When she found out how long I had been in the suicide watch cell, it was evident she was really upset. She stated that she should have been phoned within 24 hours, yet this was day five of my confinement. She stopped a passing nurse and said to her that whatever I told her was to be accepted as true. She knew I wasn't going to harm myself, so I was taken off of suicide watch. Although I was taken back to the same cell, I now had sheets and blankets.

Two days later, I was before Judge Adams and prosecutor Mark Deveraux, men whom I highly respected. Even without them speaking, I sensed a real compassion from them. I seemed to know that they tried to see my heart way beyond what had been written about me. For this, I was very thankful!

Although I did receive 11 months without probation on that day, I knew that as I allowed God to deal with me, I would truly be having a new start. Even though I wasn't actually looking forward to doing my time in federal prison, somehow, I knew it wouldn't be that bad. My growing connection with God through reading His word, the powerful dream I had, and the prayers of my Christian brothers and sisters started building hope in me. My glass was being seen as half-full now.

On the way to the Nassau County Jail, I asked the two U.S. Marshals if I could please get a shower and have something to read. They were very polite and said they would see what they could do. Back in jail, after lying down for several hours, a guard came to my cell and told me I could shower any time. I also received another blessing when the sergeant told me I would be placed with the misdemeanors, and not the felons, where I belonged. They were a lot less in numbers, and it was quieter and safer.

When I was moved from my damp cell, I was surprised that they moved me to a cell for four people, and I was the only one in there! I had much more room being alone there, without interferences, or being asked a bunch of questions about my life as a mafia wife.

The next day, I asked for a Bible to read and was given one. I began to get on my knees and started praying to God about how to handle my emotions. I was crying out to God with all my heart now. When I reached down, I opened up the Bible to Deuteronomy 8:2 in the Old Testament. I hadn't read much of the Bible, let alone the Old Testament. After wiping away my tears, I came to this passage that was speaking directly to my heart.

Remember how the Lord your God led you all the way in the desert those forty years to humble you and test you, in order to know what was in your heart.

As soon as I saw the forty years, a powerful spiritual light was turned on. The Bible seemed to have come alive to me. I crawled back upon my bed and read and read and read. It seemed I couldn't get enough of it.

The forty years passage really struck me. It had been just a few months before reading this, my father made the comment that I had been a rebellious child since the age of three. Now, at age 43, I realized that at about the age of three, I did have quite an independent spirit that grew into rebellion. It had now become seven days in jail, where I fasted, mourned, and wept. I just knew it was time for me to grow into a deeper relationship with God. My focus now was not just doing time, but to find out my true purpose in life. God had all my attention now!

Over the next few days, I ran into a few obstacles, such as the lights not working. I found a way to read in the corner, by a window. I read and read the Bible, and actually became addicted to reading it. As I poured over the pages, it seemed that the Lord often got people's attention and reached them only after one or two rough situations occurred in their lives.

Well, with me it seemed to have taken forty years. Yet, unlike the Israelites in the Old Testament, I was truly making it into the promised land! I was finally beginning to see the light from a very dark and lonely tunnel. The least I could do now, after all these years of wandering, was to hunger and thirst after Him.

I love the Lord, because He has heard my voice and my supplications. Because He has inclined His ear to me, therefore I will call upon Him as long as I live.

Psalm 116:1-2

Starting in Lowell State Prison, I can look back and see how God started me on a bread crumb trail. It seemed like from thereafter, asking Jesus to forgive me of my sins, He was giving me just enough of Him to keep me hoping and searching. When I mentioned the bread crumb trail, some said it was far-fetched, silly, or overly analytical in how I thought God moved in my life.

I read in the New Testament,

God has chosen the foolish things of the world to shame the wise.

1 Corinthians 1:27

I was really beginning not to care what people thought about me. I would rather look foolish for the Lord than remain foolish for the devil.

Like the Israelites, I, too, had to be led back through the desert for testing and restoration. I had always wanted a quick fix in life for my problems— a pill, a drink, or a snort of cocaine. These were always quick, but not a fix. My pain was lessened, but then it would return as my heart kept aching. However, the day I yielded my life over to the Lord in the suicide watch cell, much of the ache inside of me just vanished. I had been living under the sentence of death.

But now, I was living in Revelation 21:6-7.

And He said to me, "It is done! I am the Alpha and the Omega, the Beginning and the End. I will give of the fountain of the water of life freely to him who thirsts.

He who overcomes shall inherit all things, and I will be his God and he shall be My son—Jesus.

I was now hungering and thirsting for the Lord, desiring to really know my God. From my captivity to sin, to my widowhood, loss of children, and stripped of everything, to possessing all in Christ Jesus! Before, as I asked Jesus to come into my heart, I was only introduced to Him. Now, that I had turned in true repentance with a pure heart toward Him, I was really getting to know the Lord.

"Return, O backsliding children," says the Lord, "for I am married to you. I will take you, one from a city and two from a family, and I will bring you to Zion."

Jeremiah 3:14

Who would ever believe that I, Robin Colombo, could write a book and be able to show the reality of God's Word as it relates to my life? His Word says:

Do we begin again to commend ourselves? Or do we need, as some others, epistles of commendation to you or letters of commendation from you? You are our epistle written in our hearts, known and read by all men.

2 Corinthians 3:1-2

Imagine, we are living stories, walking around with people seeing the truth of God's power working in our lives. From the verses in the Bible I have shared and will share, you can see that God knew my life from the beginning, and He will see it through until the end. What love, joy, and peace this brings. In God's eyes, not only the well-known and famous get to share, but the stricken widow like me, is just as valuable. I've got so many pure dreams and desires in my heart now. My life is filled with great expectancy.

Indeed, it was for my own peace that I had great bitterness; But You have lovingly delivered my soul from the pit of corruption, for You have cast all my sins behind Your back.

For Sheol cannot thank You, death cannot praise You; Those who go down to the pit cannot hope for your truth.

Isaiah 38:17-18

Behold, God is my salvation, I will trust and not be afraid; For the Lord is my strength and song; He also has become my salvation.

Isaiah 12:2

Now, this addiction and passion for Him is the only thing that will save me spiritually, mentally, and physically. Like myself, so many wished they had come to the point of thirsting for God earlier in life. When I came to the Lord this time with my whole heart, with weeping and humility, I knew He could really start touching me. I'm not saying everyone has to come to Him with weeping and fasting, but this is what I seemed to have needed to do with such a worldly, calloused heart towards Him before.

Not only were Deuteronomy, Isaiah, and Jeremiah speaking to my heart, but so many other books of the Old Testament were, too. I see that it takes more of a desiring heart mixed with the desire of the Holy Spirit to reveal God and His truth to us. Sometimes, I just couldn't contain myself, as I would have to find someone to share what God was revealing to me. They may not have had the same degree of heart desire I had, but it only took a little on their part to make a spiritual connection, and we would both rejoice in the Lord.

One day, I was sitting on my bed in my cell when all of a sudden, a girl ran up the stairs and handed me a copy of the *Jacksonville Times-Union* newspaper. In the Lifestyle section, it had an article about the 70-year anniversary of the Monopoly game. Usually, there is a celebration at 75 or 100 years, but this was the 70th year since Monopoly began. Immediately, what raced through my mind was the fact that there were 70 co-defendants in the Monopoly scam and the captivity of Israel in Babylon was for 70 years. I tucked these facts away in my mind.

And this whole land shall be a desolation and an astonishment,
and these nations shall serve the king of Babylon seventy years.
Jeremiah 25:11

Awaiting my time to go to federal prison in Tallahassee, almost every waking moment was spent in the Bible. It seemed I kept running into the number 70 all through the Old Testament. There were 70 sons of Jezebel and Ahab.

"Now Ahab had seventy sons in Samaria. And Jehu wrote and sent letters to Samaria, to the rulers of Jezreel, to the elders, and to those who reared Ahab's sons, saying..."

2 Kings 10:1

Remember, it was earlier this same year that I was delivered from a controlling Jezebel spirit.

Also, the city of Tyre will be forgotten 70 years (Isaiah 23:15); the number of apostles was 70 that Jesus sent out to work miracles. (Luke 10:17).

Yes, all this had significance for me. I read on and on about the Jezebel spirit character. To my surprise, I found out that I had had all the characteristics of this spirit: control, deceit, manipulation, witchcraft, and others.

It was time for me now to be transported from Jacksonville to Tallahassee, and to the federal prison. My jewelry for the trip consisted of beautiful bracelets for my wrists and ankles. They differed from conventional jewelry in that, they were attached by some pretty strong chains! Imagine me, 5'1", all 110 pounds, surrounded by big, burly U.S. Marshals needing all this metal on me. Nothing like a little extra security!

We arrived at the Tallahassee airport to await a Con Air Flight. This was not a play on words, but the real name of the airline that carried prisoners to the federal prison. As the prisoners came off the plane, they were all dressed up in special security flight clothes, compliments of the B.O.P. or Bureau of Prisons.

The prisoners all looked as if they had a rough flight. There wasn't much movement on these flights, as 150 prisoners were escorted by 30 U.S. Marshals.

As I watched the faces of those getting on the bus, some friendly and some not-so-friendly, I saw a woman coming up to me whom I recognized a year earlier from Coleman Camp, in Coleman, Florida. She sat down beside me and said she's seen me someplace before. I told her where. We looked at each other to say, "Violated!" almost at the same time. We both had violated our probation, and that was why we were headed back to prison. She told me she was married, and I congratulated her.

She asked me what I'd been up to, and I looked up and said, "Ummm." I didn't want to overwhelm her, so I decided to give her the short version of my experience with the Lord. The Holy Spirit was my inspiration now, and it was so easy to share what was so joyful in my heart. I told her the good, bad, and the ugly, and told her of my complete surrender to Christ. I did not recommend that she or anyone else come to Him the way I did. There was definitely a much easier and saner way to the Lord. I guess it takes drastic measures for people who do drastic things. But now, I have come to Him, surrendering all, and have peace, such peace.

Come to Me, all you who labor and are heavy laden and I will give you rest.

Matthew 11:28

Even now, when I speak of my old life, much of it doesn't seem real.

Do not remember the former things, nor consider the things of old. Behold, I will do a new thing. Now it shall spring forth; Shall you not know it.

Isaiah 43:18-19

And that's exactly what I'm doing. I am finally able to let go of the past and my grief has truly subsided. After emptying myself out from under that cell bed, having no clothes, no food, and then weeping tears of sorrow and healing, I have come to this place in my heart where I have everything—the living God. After He emptied me, He filled me up with His word, His very presence in me. I don't have to worry about abuse, lying, cheating, and filling myself up with man-made distractions, such as drugs and alcohol. Every day now is a filling up of the Lord.

You will forget the shame of your youth, and will not remember the reproach of your widowhood anymore. For your Maker is your husband, the Lord of hosts is His name.

Isaiah 54:4

As I talked with the girl sitting beside me, the scripture in Isaiah came alive. I told her I was married to the Lord now! We both giggled, but who better to be married to than He! Neither she nor I had a Bible, as we were not allowed to carry anything during our transportation to prison. But I knew some verses, as they were so close to my heart, and shared right from there. Wow, before I even arrived at the federal prison, I was beginning to share our Lord and His Word, a joy I was able to experience with many others in the next eleven months.

CHAPTER 10

FREEDOM IN CAPTIVITY

After I was processed into the prison, the work assignment was one of the first things given. Most women have to work at least 90 days in the laundry before securing a better job in the compound. I really didn't care where I worked, and I told the Lord that. I seemed to be focusing so much on Him inside of me that I really didn't care about my outside circumstances. I would have liked to work in cosmetology, but I was told that it wouldn't start for another four months. If I had to work in the kitchen, which was the lowest rated job, I would gladly do it for the Lord. With His help, I knew no matter what, I would keep my spirits high. The inmates didn't really understand why I was so positive; therefore, I was unable to stay with one group of women for any length of time. They just couldn't understand what I'd been through and how God had delivered me out of it.

But the natural man does not understand the things of the Spirit of God, for they are foolishness to him; nor can he know them for they are spiritually discerned.

1 Corinthians 2:14

Most of the women who arrived with me had to work in the kitchen. I was waiting any day now for the call that I would have to go there, too. I kept checking the call-out list, but no job. Great! Now, I could go to the chapel on a daily basis, check out some inspirational videos for a couple of hours, and be blessed. I was able to watch the powerful film of the life of Corrie Ten Boom. She was released from a Nazi Prison Camp, and traveled around the world with the Gospel. I also liked Joyce Meyers and T.D. Jakes. I learned a lot from their teaching tapes. In addition to these, they had instructional books on the Bible, and I wanted to know all I could about them.

The women who were with me at Camp Coleman one year earlier could hardly believe the change in me. They knew me as one who was into witchcraft and who definitely didn't attend church. We had been calling on every spirit, except the Holy Spirit. It had to seem pretty amazing to them to see me so involved with church services, reading the Bible, and mostly how I was not swayed at all by other activities, such as sports and games. I was on a mission—and very determined to know all about God.

Towards the last part of June, I was given a job in the laundry. I told the Lord I would do my best and not complain. After three days, I was put on the call-out list for cosmetology. I couldn't believe it! This department was not supposed to open until September. It was only June. How could I have the job before being interviewed for it?

The new instructor was very professional in not telling anyone who got the job until we all were interviewed. I found out later that the instructor let the Holy Spirit lead her, and I got the job. What favor from God with a fellow sister! When I got the job, a few women got angry, as they received the helper positions, while I got the clerk's position. The other women had been around awhile, and I was the new kid on the cell block!

In fact, one very large woman wanted my position, and she was very outspoken about it. She said she would be the better choice because of her experience. Her name was Tony, and everything about her was big. Big voice. Big body. Big aspirations for getting my position. If the Lord had not worked in my heart to start loving people unconditionally, all 5'1" of me would have lit into her like a rabid dog. Well, if I had done that, I probably wouldn't have been here today, as she was big!

I still had to be trained for the position, even though I was a licensed cosmetologist, having learned my trade in state prison. The job entailed a lot of security responsibility. I would be in charge over all the tools and implements of the trade. There were items a lot of women would have liked to get their hands on for various reasons, as you could probably guess. Many didn't understand how a new person like me, having not earned any trust, still got the position. I was not the most liked person at that moment, but I sure was loved by my God.

It seemed like my feelings were being hurt on an hourly basis, as I could hear the snide remarks being made. I would go back to my bed at night and cry. I asked God to please help me. Soon, I turned to Exodus 14:14. It read,

The Lord will fight for you and you shall hold your peace.

I began speaking this over and over. It wasn't easy walking with God in the prison compound. My emotions were still quite fragile. It didn't take much to make me tear up and cry. But, for the most part, on a day-to-day basis, I was learning to be content and very joyful. My joy made others uncomfortable, and the fact that I didn't join them in the cursing and complaining made some of them mad. The thoughts and mindsets, along with the attitudes of the heart the Lord was developing in me, were more than enough to overcome these negative thoughts, mindsets, and bad heart attitudes I faced daily.

I knew God still had a lot of cleaning to do in my heart. Forty years of rebellious behavior needs a lot of changing. But at least I was on my way.

I think what also made others feel uneasy around me is when they started to complain about how much they had endured; they all knew I had gone through much more, and I wasn't complaining. Because of this, I found myself alone a lot by choice. I was discovering that I just didn't fit in anywhere. I just kept on checking out spiritual books from the library, reading my Bible, and always putting positive things in my mind. I can't say it enough that God's Word was such a great shield to guard my heart from all the negative attitudes, actions, and words that came at me. I didn't judge the others, for I knew they hadn't had experiences with God, the Holy Spirit, and His word.

I attended church services every Sunday. There were volunteer chaplains, as the administration was in the process of hiring a full-time one. There were only about 30 women out of 1,200 who attended services. The women said it was boring, and I had to agree that it was hard to follow. But no matter who spoke, my heart still craved hearing anyone speaking of Jesus and His word.

In July, the prison was blessed with two fine men of God. They balanced each other out well. I loved to hear Chaplain Merrill's stories of being in the Iraq war in 1991. He shared his deep feelings with us by telling us the things God was doing there. After all, this was the very land Abraham had lived in, the Garden of Eden, and the Tower of Babel. As he talked, he would make us feel as though we were there, experiencing the events just as they happened. One could feel the Bible come alive as he spoke of the land and its people.

Then there was Chaplain Minister, a very humble and truly anointed man of God. During this period, as I said before, we were so blessed with these two fine ministers of the word of God. Because of these two men, our chapel congregation started rapidly growing, to the point where we had standing room filled with about two hundred women. The Lord put together a very fine choir and musicians. He was definitely showing up, for everyone was feeling His presence.

The ministers were inviting churches from all around to be present and minister in their own unique ways. The groups included Christian Heritage Church; Straight Talk, a women's group from a radio station; the Bill Blass Prison Ministry; and the Tallahassee police department choir. Even the city police chief shared the Word in our services. We were so honored to hear them preach and sing.

One day, I was able to talk with Chaplain Minster for about ten minutes. I shared briefly with him about my past history, along with the dreams I was now having—especially the one about the ring being placed on my forefinger. Both of us immediately thought this to mean that I was a definite part of the bride of Christ.

Chaplain Minster said he believed I was on the right road, especially in diligently searching for God through His word. I also shared with him two other dreams that I had, in which I saw an open Bible where a man's hand and forefinger were going over the Scriptures. In the first dream, it was evident I was to diligently study the Lord's word. In the second dream, I was to use scripture in the writing of a book containing my life story before and after I started serving the Lord. These dreams were so important to me, for many times I thought about giving up on writing a book and bringing up the old hurts with the pain. In addition, the cosmetology instructor, who was also a sister in the Lord, encouraged me to keep writing. I just knew deep down in my heart that I was to continue to tell the story of my life and the Lord's great work in me.

After these dreams, I completely started over with the book and began to bring scripture into it that was parallel to my life. At first, it wasn't easy for me to read God's word when I was the bad guy in the story. What at first seemed impossible, in getting the facts and real thoughts of my life out on paper, became pretty easy as I asked the Lord for guidance. Now, the book took on a whole new meaning when using more of God's word, because He showed me the reality of my life and where I was headed. After surrendering all to Him, I saw how walking with God and His truth started becoming my reality. Everything was now beginning to flow easily. What an Almighty God!

I really didn't have any idea about how to go about getting my book published. Sometime in July, I wrote to a few publishing ministries, but got no replies. I wrote to the publisher of Dr. Gill, and they wrote back saying they were a private publisher for him only. They were named Love Press and had a heart on the outside of the envelope. The heart stuck out to me, and I kept thinking of it. As you will see, it played an important part in the publishing of this book. Love Press did send me a couple of addresses of publishing companies, and as they wrote back, they asked me to write a short statement about the contents of the book. The only thing I could say was how God brought me out of a living hell. Having received no responses from them, I put my writing down for a short time.

I didn't put my Bible down, however, nor my zeal for God, which was burning on the inside of me. Nothing was going to interfere with my new life with God. Nothing! I had to separate myself from many people I cared about. Not that I stopped loving them, but our friendships weren't moving in the same direction. There were difficult decisions for me, and I didn't want people to think I was rejecting them, but some of their attitudes, actions, and words could really affect my heart in a negative way.

My physical condition was not great, as I was wearing the conventional inmate fashion and tennis shoes with holes in them. The little money I had was running out, and the pay scale of my work in the prison was the lowest of all. Although they housed and fed you, money was needed for other things. Yet, I kept the spiritual goals intact that God had given me through the scripture, dreams, and other godly people.

Not long after, I started seeing the blessing of the Lord. One woman gave me her new sweatsuit as she was leaving prison. I got some new shoes, and, then, I got a pay raise at work, plus two bonuses. Usually, you only got one bonus—if any at all. One day, I even signed my paycheck for one amount, went to the teller machine, and somehow received extra money. People on the outside were sending me money.

I was beginning to truly like the person that God was changing me into. I was learning not to sweat the small stuff. Although I still liked nice things, I found that I was just as satisfied with what I'd been given.

That you put off, concerning your former conduct, the old man which grows corrupt according to the deceitful lusts, and be renewed in the spirit of your mind, and that you put on the new man which was created according to God, in true righteousness and holiness.

Ephesians 4:22-24

This new person the Lord was making me into was a peaceful person, really resting in the living God. I didn't focus on the physical things anymore, but the supernatural. I was beginning to really know that all my provision came from Him. I now stood on the promises of His word, and unlike the other godfather, I was serving and connected to God the Father!

During my free time, I continued reading the Bible. The scriptures kept leaping into my heart. Again, I was able to see how the verse of the Bible pointed to my life so directly. As I became closer and closer to God, my life's purpose became clear. From my life and the scripture, I wanted to share with as many as possible the reality of God. He warns us of the dangers we face and the powerful forces that are ever-ready to destroy us. Yet, at the same time, I could share of His all-conquering power!

Be sober, be vigilant; because your adversary the devil walks about like a roaring lion, seeking whom he may devour.

I Peter 5:8

Behold, I give you the authority to trample on serpents and scorpions, and all the power of the enemy, and nothing shall by any means hurt you.

Luke 10:19

A person who hasn't broken man's laws and ended up in prison could actually be in a worse prison in his heart through hate, anger, bitterness, and unforgiveness. These things will lock out the true blessings of God from us and our families. I know from experience that if God can restore me and my family, He not only can, but desires to restore everyone else.

Later in July of 2005, I was moved to a new wing. My new bunkies or bunkmates were two women from Colombia. They had been heads of drug cartels before being incarcerated; one for life. In Central and South America, a woman could be the leader of a drug ring, but not so in the Italian Mafia. Men were the only head honchos. I mentioned to them about my desire to publish a book that I was working on. One of the women showed me a business card of a movie production company that wanted to make a movie about her life. The company was called Milk & Honey. This is reminiscent of the land of milk and honey the Lord wanted to take the Israelites into in the Old Testament. By sharing the card with me, it gave me that much more incentive to publish my book and tell the story of what God did in my life. When I left them, I turned to the book of Deuteronomy and came right to the passage where God wanted to lead his people into the Promised Land, which reads:

For the Lord your God is God of gods and Lord of lords, the great God, mighty and awesome, who shows no partiality nor takes a bribe.
He administers justice for the fatherless and the widow, and loves the stranger, giving him food and clothing.

Deuteronomy 10:17-18

When I read this with tears streaming down my face, I knew in my heart what God was calling me to do. He was impressing upon me to keep pressing on and to tell all the people how much He loved them. I was a widow twice over, and at this moment, these scriptures were becoming so alive and real to me. I sobbed for two hours and felt such indescribable love and compassion from God. My bunkmates just let me cry, for they sensed my true love for God and His love for me. I knew a great cleansing was taking place in me with the flow of tears. I had cried so many hopeless tears before I became a Christian. Now, my heart was full of hope and expectation.

As I read on in the Old Testament, I kept finding the number 70. I asked the Lord to please show me the significance of this number. Even a few of my friends couldn't wait until I received the answer. Several months passed. Finally, I found the answer. Just as before, with the 70-year anniversary of the Monopoly game and 70 co-defendants, God showed me in Zechariah 12:1, that He would end my captivity soon, as He did for the Israelites after 70 years. This was revealed to me on October 29th, 2005.

From where I was sitting, how could I not take heed of God's word? I learned such a lesson from this as I had once told my daughter, when her father died, to read only the New Testament, since the Old Testament couldn't relate to us. How wrong I was. I'm glad she didn't listen to me. It is the whole word of God that delivers. I don't need the mob's protection. I've got God's word right here.

We can be the recipients of God's love. When I say can, it simply means we have the choice of opening our hearts and receiving His love. So, it is with all my heart that I urge people not to wait like I did, until they lose a loved one, or lose their freedom in prison, or maybe come near to losing their sanity. Even worse, waiting until you are in bondage with drugs, alcohol, or the love of a man or woman you entirely depend on. As you read earlier, I put my trust in astrologers and fortune tellers. I thought it was all innocent, but I was truly deceived.

Let now the astrologers and stargazers and monthly prognosticators stand up and save you from what shall come upon you.

Isaiah 47: 13

I experienced the utter lack of help from the astrologers and fortune tellers. These were just traps of Satan and his deceptive lies that have captured so many. Now, I am captured by the love of Christ!

Reflections

As I sit here diligently reading and studying hard, I am seeking with all my heart and soul to learn as much as possible about the Lord and His word. I have done this not only for myself, but to help bring understanding to many others. It just dawned on me that just as God used the life of Joseph, where his brothers sold him into slavery, God used that situation to bless many in Joseph's family and in Egypt as well (Genesis 45:5). This so parallels my own life, because as I sold myself into the slavery of sin and man's ways, my life is now touching many—even some of my family members and inmates. Glory be to God, as He turned what was a devastating situation into an over-abundance of blessing to others. God has made it possible for me to find wisdom to write of His life through my own experiences. He has placed His favor upon me in a physical prison to have the supplies, biblical resources, and time alone to place my life and thoughts down, so many will receive His life and direction for themselves.

Who comforts us in all our tribulation that we may be able to comfort those who are in any trouble, with the comfort with which we ourselves are comforted by God.

2 Corinthians 1:4

In the last several months, God has given me a design of a building to have a beauty salon. It will be a Christian-based salon, called Heavenly Hands and Hair. It is my hope to open this in Jacksonville with God's total help. Also, an idea came to me and a friend about an animated movie featuring contraband veggies as the characters. I wanted to include some of my family in the story. The only thing missing was a name for the movie. After praying for about ten minutes, the name "Contoons" came into my mind.

The Lord has given me work to do for Him to reach people, such as this book, and a potential movie. These are big projects, yet I want to be faithful in the small things also, reaching that one person the Lord has placed in front of me.

He who is faithful in what is least is faithful also in much; and he who is unjust in what is least is unjust also in much.

Luke 16:10

When I stopped trying to keep control of my own life and turned everything over to the Lord, then things were so much easier and started coming together. The Lord wanted to be a part of my everyday life and decisions, so that my life would be fuller on this earth, this side of heaven. When I started allowing Him to be part of my daily life and work things out for me, then powerful scripture began to come alive.

And then they will know that I am the Lord.

Jeremiah 24:7

After I received revelation after revelation about demonic spirits and how real they are, I was practically running to my inmate buddies to share with them. However, they patronized me and kind of patted me on the back saying, "Okay, Colombo, good going." I desperately wanted to express to them just how real and dangerous demonic spirits were, especially the Jezebel spirit and the spirits of deception. The Jezebel spirit would try to manipulate men to get what she wanted. This spirit, through people, will lie, steal, and commit fraud, all for self-serving purposes. I know, because I have been there and done it.

Nevertheless, I have a few things against you, because you allow that woman Jezebel, who calls herself a prophetess, to teach and seduce My servants to commit sexual immorality and eat things sacrificed to idols.

And I gave her time to repent of her sexual immorality, and she did not repent.

Indeed, I will cast her into a sickbed, and those who commit adultery with her into great tribulation, unless they repent of their deeds.

Revelation 2:20-22

The deceiving spirit is horrific, and its purpose is to destroy all sound judgment and cause people to believe a lie and live a life of deception. Those who are deceived don't know they're deceived, because they are deceived! This spirit distorts reality in a person's mind, and they begin rationalizing that evil is good. I knew that these spirits were working in me by my persistent lifestyle. As I search the scriptures, I found the names of these spirits in the Old and New Testament. I also knew that these spirits could not just begin working in you, for you had to open yourself up to them by committing their respective acts of sin. Once this is done on a consistent basis, these spirits enter and operate on your mind, will, and emotions—and take on a part of your personality. This is what happened to me until I was delivered by the Holy Spirit through some godly people. These demons would progress, projecting their thoughts into my mind by actually speaking to me. I could hear their voices saying, "You'll never amount to anything. You've always been like this. You'll never change." Then, I started to live up to what these voices said. I was in a spiral of defeat and degradation and didn't really know it.

I so remember Chaplain Minster saying, "God's word has power." That is why I would read it more and more and start to speak it out. Two scriptures come to mind that back these statements up. The first one is:

For the word of God is living and powerful, and sharper than any two-edged sword, piercing even to the division of soul and spirit, and of joints and marrow, and is a discerner of the thoughts and intents of the heart.

Hebrews 4:12

I want my words to edify and build up those who are receiving it. Not destroy. There are so many words I wish I could take back. Words that I spoke to my late husband in anger and frustration. It's too late to take them back after they are gone. The tongue can have such a positive or negative affect on our lives. Gossiping and cursing are quick to damage the human heart. Pleasant, godly words build up people.

Matthew 12:34-35 states:

Brood of vipers! How can you, being evil, speak good things? For out of the abundance of the heart the mouth speaks. A good man out of the good treasure of his heart brings forth good things, and an evil man out of the evil treasure brings forth evil things.

If I am to have a treasure of good things in my heart, then I must be daily storing up good things in my heart. In contrast, if I have bad things come out of my mouth, it must have come from a storehouse of those bad things of the world and sinful nature. I store up things in my heart with my thoughts, attitudes, actions, and words. It hit me so hard that we are constantly storing up things, good or bad, every day of our lives!

For forty years, I was storing up horrendous things. Looking back over the early incidences in my life, specifically four bad experiences, there were many things that were preparing my heart to be set up for more misery and pain. The first three were perpetrated upon me by others, and they caused hurt and a spiritually damaged heart at an early age. For instance, my pet dog, Frisky, was taken from me only to be followed up by the killing of my baby lamb. Then, there was the evil man who tried to sexually assault me. Finally, the fourth thing I did was to get involved with a Ouija board, which quickly brought upon me the visible sights of spirits above my door. However innocent this may have been done on my part, it opened up grave habits and dangers later on in life. I warn people now to not get involved in any form of magic and witchcraft and to get healed from any hurts that have entered their hearts by their own sin or the sin of others.

On October 2nd, 2005, Chaplain Minster invited all the inmates in the Chapel that day to write down on a piece of paper all the things they had ever done wrong. Once that was done, they were to bring the pieces of paper to the altar, crumple them up, and throw them away. He then would pray over us individually. It took some of us an hour, but we wanted to be thorough. What a wonderful and powerful action that was for us that day! We were actually casting our past into the pit, and our past would no longer have any effect on our present or our future lives.

Chaplain Minster anointed my head with oil and prophesied over me. He told me that I would be a well-known woman of God. He also said that my blessings would multiply in comparison with all my past sins. From where I was sitting, it represented a tremendous number of blessings! These prophesies impacted me to redirect my life with great purpose in the writing of this book. The book would be a tool to bless and minister to others from all walks of life. As I saw it, the multiplied blessings would be to see thousands find our Lord and Savior, Jesus Christ.

Before coming to Christ, I would try to manipulate people to get external things to fill my heart with love. How ironic that the circumstances of prison, which could have produced misery in my life, now gave me plenty of time to seek our Lord Jesus and for Him to fill my heart!

Being in prison with women from all over the world who were practicing white magic, as well as black magic, I saw them calling up the dead. Some very heavy Haitian voodoo was also practiced. Yet, I had no fear of these things affecting me, because I was protected by the power of Jesus Christ.

Having disarmed principalities and powers, He made a public spectacle of them, triumphing over them in it.

Colossians 2:15

Since a major part of prison is Satan's playground, I can still hear the fear and defeat of others who are living in the negative and destructive environment the devil so freely provides. Powerful words denote such a hopeless heart of existence. My heart so goes out to them, yet I just quietly but firmly rebuke those words in the name of Jesus, so as not to allow them to enter my heart. Even several months back, when I didn't have the knowledge of the power of Jesus' name, the Lord would speak His written word to my heart. One example clearly comes to mind. One day, I was being attacked with words while at work in my regular prison job. I couldn't get a grip on my emotions, so I ran to my bunk and wanted to scream. I couldn't. So, I grabbed a pen and paper and wrote, "God, help!" My heart broke. "Comfort me quickly, I need you. It's difficult being human. It's too painful! I hate Satan. I despise him!" When I opened my Bible for words of comfort, I turned to:

"I know you by name, and you have also found grace in my sight." And He said, "My presence will go with you, and I will give you rest."

Exodus 33:12,14

It was becoming quite clear to me, the closer we were to God, Satan tried even harder to work on us. With me, I had given him so many areas of my life. He would try to then hit me, especially in those same areas. It didn't mean I never got depressed or grieved. It just meant that with the word of God and the use of Jesus' name, I was becoming stronger in overcoming those areas through the exercise of my faith, and witnessing the overcoming victory of Jesus in my life.

In my weakness, He was made strong.
Hebrews 11:34

On Easter Sunday of 2005, I watched the uncut version of the movie *The Passion of the Christ* for the first time. After seeing the graphic reality of what Jesus endured with the scourging and crucifixion, I wiped away a flood of tears from my eyes. Then, I removed the cross I wore around my neck, knowing I was not worthy to wear it. I never realized the significance or the impact of how watching the brutal slaughter of the black baby lamb, my pet forty years ago, would affect me in seeing the brutal and merciless slaying of the Lamb of God that could save us from our sins. As a child, I had seen the precious lamb that meant so much to me being slain and causing a deep stain in my heart. Now, as a child of God, watching *The Passion of the Christ*, I knew He took all the stains of sin, hurt, and wounds for all mankind. Glory to the Son of God!

He was oppressed and He was afflicted, yet He opened not His mouth; He was led as a lamb to the slaughter, and as a sheep before its shearers is silent, so He opened not His mouth.
Isaiah 53:7

During the eleven months of being incarcerated in federal prison,

I found it was not like being in prison at all. Yes, I was locked up and behind bars and restricted in my movements, but because I had truly turned my life over to Christ and turned my back completely on my old life by repentance, I was truly free in my heart. I was allowing the Lord to work out the sin in my life and at the same time building myself up in Him and really experiencing the presence of God in me. Believe me, this is what made the big difference in this prison, as opposed to the state prison. A difference as daylight is to darkness.

As I've said before, the Lord favored me with a clerk's job and a godly supervisor all day long. I wasn't bombarded all the time with complaining and anger from the inmates. The cosmetology supervisor was a Christian, and her gentle spirit was in great contrast to most inmates. The Lord also favored me (Psalms 5:12) with the officers by granting me the privilege of going into private rooms adjoining the chapel. I would spend hours in these private rooms viewing Christian videos that really ministered to me. Another great factor in my time in federal prison was the bunkmates in my cubicle.

Two wonderful blessings I want to share with you were my two bunkmates, Mery Valencia and Paula Woods. They have given me permission to use their real names. They had been two powerful women in the drug trade. Mery was the lord of a mega drug ring out of Colombia. She lived in the United States. Paula, an African-American, met with the Colombian cartel once they came to the United States and helped with the operations here. Besides handling drugs, both ran respectable and legitimate businesses in the United States. Like Paula, Mery came from a very good family and was well-educated. They lived in nice neighborhoods, had children, and were soccer moms. Their lives were very normal on the surface. Not in your wildest dreams would you have guessed their main line of work. They both have hearts of gold. Mery inherited her husband's drug business when he died. Paula just got caught up in the lifestyle and couldn't easily get out. They've been given a lot of time for non-violent crimes, but because of the positions they held, they were given life sentences.

At this time, both are appealing for reduced time. These women are not like the movie types, hard and callous. Actually, after having lived with them for almost a year, I saw them willing to wipe away somebody else's tears quicker than their own. I have known them as people living their lives to be givers and not to be takers like so many others. I asked both of them to share an interesting time in their life. The two incidences they shared seemed to have really awakened them up to the reality of the life they were leading.

I will start with Mery Valencia. Since getting caught going to a festival in Brazil from Colombia in 2000, Mery has been in federal prison. The U.S. did not have an extradition treaty with Colombia, so the feds had to wait until somebody tipped them off about Mery visiting Brazil. She looks like a Liz Claiborne or Ralph Lauren model and got caught up in the love of money and power. With a very smart head on her shoulders, she capitalized on her late husband's business. She was not a dangerous woman, but shrewd, waiting for people to approach her about the business, and never approaching them.

One of the stories she shared with me about her drug business was amusing. It probably made her wise as to how the feds were closing in on her and why she probably should move to Colombia. One time, while in the States, being in charge of a lot of money and mega amounts of cocaine, she decided to go check on an apartment where a lot of the drugs were kept. As soon as she arrived, she looked out the window and saw the police everywhere. She told her dealers she needed to get to another floor and quick. As she opened the door of the apartment, she faced the police, who said, "Freeze."

Seeing her life flash before her eyes, she coolly and politely said, "What is the problem, officers?" They told her not to move. By this time, Mery was trying to remember her attorney's telephone number.

But, in an amazing twist of fate, the police were in the process of busting the apartment next door, a bust on a much smaller scale than hers. After Mery picked up her heart off the floor, she was out of there. She then changed her place of operation and told her guys never to call her to check on anything again. She would only manage the money and direct the trafficking of drugs.

A few things I mention now will show you the kind of person Mery is. Several years ago, she was approached by a producer who wanted to make the best of her situation while in prison. This would be by helping people along the way. She declined, not wanting to glamorize the criminal lifestyle. Another time, I didn't ask her to make me a birthday cake and decorate my bunk, but she did anyway. Mery also gave me a brand-new pair of tennis shoes to replace my holey ones! She is touching many lives in many ways while she is in prison. Shortly after telling me this story, I felt led to share some scriptures with her. I watched her intently as I shared with her, and she appeared keenly interested. I followed up with her the very next day and asked her if she read the verses of scripture. She said she had. She stated that she was really moved by Psalms 55. She was particularly touched by verses 12, 13, and 14, since they reminded her about a friend who betrayed her. Someone had to snitch on her whereabouts in going to Brazil.

When Satan starts using someone to get at you and you want to lash out at them, read Psalms 55, as I did at such a time. I felt such a rush of peace and calm come over me, so much so that tears ran down my cheeks.

I am so glad that God gave me a heart of compassion when I came to Him, changing my heart of stone. I am now able to see people's hearts clearly, and I could see Mery had a humble heart and wasn't haughty.

The other bunkmate, Paula Woods, is the one who met with the Colombian cartel once they reached the States. Paula was a very pretty African-American woman, intelligent, and not a flashy type. Looking at her, you would think she was *the girl next door* and not one who was high up in the drug trade. The experience she shared with me that really impacted her life took place in a small town in Florida, called Barth. It was a one-light type of town with not much going on, except a good-size drug trade. Paula was mostly responsible for that happening. Kids were running all over the streets with no shoes on. The buildings were dilapidated. In fact, the whole town was almost in shambles. She knew the cause of the demise of this town—the drug trade, which thrived there. It was a nice little town at one time, and now it looked like a ghost town of the Old West. Paula once made a remark to one of the drug dealers, stating how their trade had brought on the destitution of the place. He just looked at her and said she was crazy.

What happened to Paula on that day was her eyes were opened to the destruction she helped to bring upon the town and its people. There was no more rush or thrill for her in this business. She had been raised a Christian, and I'm sure, with a praying mother and grandmother, her conscience really began to bother her.

Paula did relate one other story to me, even though it took a hilarious turn. It goes to illustrate the truth in the word of God that your sins will find you out (Numbers 32:23).

One day, Paula and her dealers were traveling along in a convoy of two cars and a minivan with a shipment of cocaine. Since they were traveling on the interstate, they decided to put their stash behind the dashboard for security purposes. However, as they were traveling along, one of the guys thought he'd smoke a little marijuana. Not very long after they had lit up, their car was pulled over by a state trooper for a routine check. The guys quickly decided to turn on the air vents to clear the odor out. *Big mistake!* When they turned the vents full blast, it exploded the cocaine bags. All the cocaine blew out and now covered the dealers' hair, beards, and clothes. This made the state trooper's job really easy. Paula's son, who followed behind their car, suspected some trouble with the others being pulled over. They later found out the details of the arrest, when they talked with them in jail.

Later on, when Paula got busted, she told me she breathed a sigh of relief, as the whole drug racket was beginning to make her emotionally and mentally sick. At the time of her arrest, she was living in a respectable neighborhood, with everyday Americans who got up and went to work at their regular jobs.

A lot of the big drug lords don't live on the streets and out in the open. They aren't flashing a lot of gold and hip-hopping around on street corners. The movies and music today glorify these young men and women, but they are the *small potatoes* used by the drug kings to pawn their passion of drugs.

The higher Paula went up the drug ladder operations, the more miserable she became. This took a toll on her personal life. She didn't know who to trust anymore. Paula is very remorseful about her past. Now, she is committed to helping those around her in federal prison.

As I have said before, I found favor with God in federal prison, having arrived there after I had committed my whole heart to Him. I couldn't be doubleminded anymore (James 1:6), especially in here. Being fully committed to the Lord, I was able to draw the utmost of His help and strength. I called out to God for grace and mercy, knowing He would answer, for my heart was fully toward Him. One powerful scripture that motivated me during my days here was in Jeremiah 29:13-14, which reads:

And you will seek Me and find Me, when you search for Me with all your heart. I will be found by you and I will bring you back from your captivity.

This is for anyone who is in any type of captivity to sin. God is no respecter of persons, for He will deliver anyone who comes to Him and will keep on delivering them as they seek and serve Him first. One of the great truths of God I have learned in my seeking is to treat the Holy Spirit living in me as a divine person, which He is. He is called the very Spirit of Christ in Philippians 1:19. It's incredible that the living God made His home in me the very second I received Jesus as Lord and Savior. I desired the Holy Spirit to control my will, mind, and emotions. This total yielding to Him brings such pleasure. Our Heavenly Father has sent to us who believe, the blessed Holy Spirit to bring us into a close relationship with Him.

On January 26th, 2006, I wrote down a dream I had the previous night. I was flying in the air and then started hovering over a pond and ravine. I saw a huge alligator, a swimming monkey, and a turtle. In my dream, I knew the place was my parents' property, and I landed down by some trees. I heard a very loud galloping sound and hid behind a tree to peer in the direction of the galloping. I saw a brown, white, red, and black horse running very hard, so I stayed behind the tree, for fear of being trampled. When I awoke, I wondered why I had so many dreams of horses galloping. I assumed it was because of my love of horses.

A little after I awakened, my bunkmate decided to clean the floor, so I grabbed my Bible and a chair and positioned myself in the hallway. When I opened my Bible, it was in Zechariah, chapter one. When I got to verse eight it stated,

I saw by night, and behold a man riding on a red horse and it stood among the myrtle trees in the hollow; and behind him were horses: red, sorrel (brown) and white.

Now, I'm totally captivated and want to scream out in excitement because of the similarities in Zechariah's vision and my dream. I read on down to verse 17, where it read,

Again, proclaim, saying, thus says the Lord of hosts. My cities shall again spread out through prosperity. The Lord will again comfort Zion, and again will choose Jerusalem.

I wept and cried, for my heart could hardly believe what I had just taken in. As I've studied the Old Testament, the Lord has had me place myself in identity with Zion. Everywhere Zion is mentioned, the Spirit of God is speaking of me and all true believers. In my study

Bible, I looked over to the next page, of Zechariah 2:7-9, where it reads:

Up Zion, you who dwell with the daughter of Babylon (sinful world), for thus says the Lord of hosts. He sent Me after glory to the nations who plunder you; for he who touches you touches the apple of His eye. For surely, I will shake my hand against them.

The *apple of God's eye* is the godly remnant who will receive His favor and His love. A note in the margin of my study Bible read, "The bride being prepared for His Son." It all came flooding back to me as I recalled one of the darkest hours of my life. This was when I stayed under the metal bed in the suicide watch cell, for three days with no clothes, food, or drink. It was the dream I had about a large hand placing a wedding ring on my finger. We are engaged to Christ:

For I am jealous for you with godly jealously. For I have betrothed you to one husband, that I may present you as a chaste virgin to Christ.

2 Corinthians 11:2

If anyone is now living in Babylon, with witchcraft, lies, and worldly affection, now is the time to escape.

Zechariah 2:7

At this time, the Lord showed me about Solomon—with all his riches and wisdom—yet his kingdom was on its way to destruction with his sons. Solomon chose to build his own kingdom so lavishly and almost forsook God. Solomon really went his own way for much of his life and didn't seek God with a fervent heart. I could see so clearly that those of this present time with riches and wisdom and without God, will come to nothing.

My Spiritual Friend, Amanda

Not only did the Lord show me favor with my job, the officers on duty, as well as my private time in the chapel, but He blessed me with a very dear friend with whom I had a lot in common. It turned out that Amanda and I had both been in the state prison at Lowell together. Although we didn't know each other, we knew the same people. Several years later, we were to meet in federal prison in Tallahassee. I have learned that there are no coincidences with God.

One day, Amanda and I were on routine doctor visits in the medical center. All the seats were taken, so I was forced to take a seat on the floor. Being the petite woman that I am, that was no problem. I knew ahead of time that the wait could be an all-day affair, so I went prepared, having my Bible, notebook, and a couple of spiritual books. I wasn't concerned about the stares I was receiving from others by carrying all this around with me. At this point, I only cared what God thought, and He would take care of the rest. I was on a mission! As I was sitting there, Amanda, also being petite, asked me if she could squeeze in beside me. I said yes, of course. We openly discussed our beliefs and our love for Jesus. Then, we found out we had much more in common. Later that night, as I pondered over my encounter with Amanda, I just knew it was the Lord who arranged for us to meet. It was not easy finding someone to partner with inside a prison, particularly in a commitment to attend church regularly. God blessed Amanda and my relationship abundantly as we attended many services together, missing only a few, and really going after God. She and I would comment to one another, "I love the way you love God."

With all our defenses down, we wore no masks, and were in total surrender to the Lord Jesus Christ. Oh, what freedom this brought! It was so different from all the pretenses in a world where you hide all the secrets, pain, and misery of the heart. The Lord already knows everything in our hearts, and we both knew this, as we became totally open in allowing Him to remove anything in us that was not of Him. I cherished the moments during the services when we could kneel down and bow our heads at the altar, not caring who was watching. It was just us and our Lord Jesus Christ, giving and receiving His unconditional love. Oh! The tears of love for Him at this time more than made up for the tears of pain we both experienced in the past.

As you can see, federal prison was totally different than the state system. First of all, my whole heart was given to Jesus, and I allowed Him, as I said before, to remove sin and attitude that were contrary to His very nature. Second, the Lord deposited so much of His word deep inside of me, that His presence became so real in my heart all the time. This captivity in prison allowed me to pray, read, reflect, share Him, and honor Him in a place where the environment opposes such actions. This just goes to show you the power and majesty of the living God. My heart's prayer is that, if you do not know the Lord Jesus Christ, you will come to know Him in all His fullness. No matter what you've done or your situation in life, He can take your life and make you free from the inside out. Won't you open your heart to Him today?

Robin L. Colombo

was born in the 60s, and in the 60s, you didn't go see a psychiatrist. To do so was unheard of – if you did actually go and seek someone out to help you with your issues, you were considered "crazy". My mother suffered from bipolar disorder, and she flat-out refused to get diagnosed – with anything - because her generation was even worse than mine. They didn't talk about things like mental health and looking after one's emotional wellbeing. As a result of being raised by a generation that refused to look any harder into their problems than they needed to, I went undiagnosed well into my thirties. I started off searching for help with my first psychiatrist, and he never mentioned bipolar—he was just throwing medications at me, pills meant to treat things like anxiety and depression.

That was the only relief I would receive from what I was going through for many, many, years. I would rarely get anything more from other psychiatrists; depression medications, many depression medications, and, for me, they didn't work. I lived my life like this, and figured that I would do so indefinitely, until one year, I was in Macon, Georgia, and I hit the wall of what I could and could not take. I realized that there was no way that I could live like that anymore. I couldn't sleep – I wouldn't sleep for days on end, my mind racing from one thought to the next. It was like there was a vicious whirlwind in my brain. The way that my thoughts would chase each other felt like a game of ping-pong I was playing against myself, constantly, on my own, and struggling through it in silence.

I got out the phonebook to find a psychiatrist. In my endless searching, I came across a bipolar specialist. I didn't know what this "specialist" did – in Jacksonville, there were no such specialists, and I had never heard of a bipolar specialist before. I didn't know how to reach out, afraid that I would simply receive another prescription for another pill that did not work. At that point, I had been on ten years of medications that made me even crazier. Not one medication had worked for me. Each time I would get handed a new one, I would feel a tiny flutter of something like hope, thinking that maybe this would be the pill that would quiet my mind down and help me get through my days. Each time, I was only disappointed again. When they inevitably didn't work for me, it made me feel as though there was no hope, and that there would never be any, at least not for me. The doctors were not getting it; they didn't hear me, or maybe they weren't really listening, when I told them that the things that they were prescribing me did not help. I don't think they knew what to do with me at that point.

So, when I finally went to see this bipolar specialist, such relief came over me, so much hope, because I was in despair. To get ready to go see him, I went three days with no caffeine. I left my bedroom door open all weekend and drank water the entire time, as much as I could consume. When Monday came, the day of my appointment with the specialist, I was so eager to get to him that I was in tears the entire time that I drove to his office. I was still expecting the same kind of psychiatrist that I had been seeing, I was expecting that once again, nothing would change, but still, I had hope.

When I arrived at his office, and he called me inside, he took one look at me, and he knew what to prescribe me. He was absolutely a specialist; while medication can normally take a few weeks to get into your system and begin taking effect, the medication he gave me had me feeling better in just two days. Five years later, I am still on that same medication.

As you've read the book, you've seen where I've tried to commit suicide. In my life, I have had three major attempts to end my suffering and my misery. These were not just superficial wounds; I once had a paring knife all the way to the wood in my throat, just missing my carotid artery. I took multiple pill cocktails, ones that have killed many people, but they didn't kill me. I survived those attempts and woke up an hour after taking them. The last time that that happened was when I went for the knife, because I was so mad that I was still alive and in the world. People who really want to commit suicide are often mad when they wake up - I was no exception. My anger at still being alive was visceral. In my mind, I had done so many bad things against the law, although I didn't believe that I had ever directly harmed anyone. I didn't steal from people, but I liked to shoplift. I became a shopaholic. I made choices driven by money sometimes, and those choices weren't always exactly legal.

When you're given anti-depressants by a psychiatrist, you usually think that you're not supposed to be depressed anymore. But when you're not given the right cocktail for bipolar disorder, those anti-depressants are not going to work. I once told one of my psychiatrists to just take my brain out, study it, and get back to me. I know it's not just me who suffers like this; I know that there are hundreds of thousands of people suffering from this same disease, and, like me, they are suffering in silence. But there's nothing to be ashamed of. There is a magic cocktail out there for those of us with Bipolar I disorder. I'm not saying that taking pills is going to make you feel like a million dollars every day, but you will have far more good days than bad days. You will get off the rollercoaster. My advice to those of you who are suffering is to find not just a psychiatrist, but a bipolar specialist. I found mine in Macon, Georgia. His name is Dr. Ahmandi, and he changed my life.

Looking back now, I know that God had a hand in that as well, because he saw how much I was suffering and knew I did not want to live like that anymore. The only reason I quit my suicide attempts is because of the attempt that I had made that didn't work, though they should have: I was afraid that I would do just enough damage to myself that I would be brain dead or paralyzed, and I wasn't sure what would happen in the afterlife if I committed suicide.

Finally, I've now come to see the love my children and grandchildren have for me, and though I've never felt needed before - or even wanted - I've come to know the love of those around me that love me, and they have made me feel needed and wanted and told me I have a mission on this earth. Truly I must, otherwise I don't think that I would still be here. I am God's instrument now, one that He can use for good, to come out about this disease and hope that my story helps others who suffer as I have suffered.

In hindsight, I am so grateful to so many people, but especially to God. He heard my cries, my tears, and though I couldn't see it fourteen years ago, I was told that it was going to be in God's time. God has taken my tragedies and, where another person may have died, He has kept me alive. You would think that I would have been grateful back then, but I wasn't. I was not grateful at all. I couldn't see the light.

To me, personally - I would like to reiterate that I'm talking about me, personally—to me, no light was visible. I would be on my knees praying, crying, and begging God to take me home. It was too hard for me here, in this life. I didn't feel as though I had anything to give to society anymore or to my children. I was certain that I would bring nothing but pain to everyone around me. I know that people often use the word "crazy" very loosely, and I laugh with them when the do, but I don't feel that I'm crazy. I just can't keep my emotions or my sleeping habits in check on my own, that's all. When you stay up for days at a time on a regular basis, it's pure torture.

All that said, I felt like an outcast. I wanted to just tuck myself away in my room. I would think to God, "Well, I guess this is how I'll stay out of trouble and live my days. This is it." That's how I felt in Georgia, when I finally hit the point that I knew I had to reach out to someone, anyone. I felt that I was too old to start a new career, and the more dramatic that the things happening to me in my life became, the worse my bipolar became. Dramatic events escalated it. Stress and traumatic happenings in your life can make your bipolar worsen.

I'm having more good days now, today, because I can see the light. That light for me is this book, because I'm hoping that enough people will get it into their hands, and it will help them realize they're not alone in anything. That there's more of us who are suffering. On that note, I bid you to please seek out professional help. Don't be ashamed to do so, and don't be ashamed of needing it, if you do. If you don't want anyone to know, don't tell them. Go on your own. You will be amazed how, with the right medication, you can live a productive life, one that is defined more by its highs than its lows.

Now that I'm on the right medication for me, I don't see suicide as an option. Of course, even though I'm on the perfect medication for myself, it's not a fix-all every day. I still have my lows and highs. The events of my life still affect me. The difference is that now, taking my medication as directed (I used to think *maybe if I take another one it will help more*) when I do have my low days and don't want to get out of bed, suicide isn't an option for me anymore. For me, that is huge. Good luck to you!

EPILOGUE

When the waves of death surrounded me, the floods of ungodliness made me afraid. The sorrows of Sheol surrounded me, the snares of death confronted me. In my distress I called upon the Lord, and cried out to my God; He heard my voice from His temple, and my cry entered His ears.

Psalms 18:5

I chose this particular scripture for the epilogue because it sums up exactly what happened. You personally may not have gone through all that I have, but if you can relate to anything I have written, then I recommend that you write this scripture down and read it out loud to God's ear.   It's so powerful, the angels and the devil hear it and recognize it as being true.

I've been asked the question, "How did you feel when leaving the prison?" My response is simple. Because I felt so much freedom in prison, I didn't feel any different. I didn't feel the need to go to any particular place or to do anything special, except to visit with friends and family. I guess you could say I was feeling a lot like the Apostle Paul, who was content in any situation.

...and I know how to be abased, and I know how to abound. Everywhere and in all things I have learned both to be full and to be hungry, both to abound and suffer need.

Philippians 4:12

Before coming out of prison, I did have the fear of losing the closeness I felt with God on the inside. I would pray diligently for my children's peace, salvation, and happiness. What I didn't know was God was already answering and on top of things. My daughter, Jennifer, was given an excellent job with a fine boss, who is a cosmetic dentist. This dentist loves the Lord. She ended up working on my teeth at no charge. My grandson, Tyler, has been offered record deals for his rapping. He goes by the name Sluggatee.

As for my son, Frankie, he is engaged to a beautiful woman named Maddie. They have an 18-month-old little girl named Lila. I'm a big part of my children's lives, and I enjoy seeing my grandchildren grow up. Although my husband is deceased, I can still call Mr. and Mrs. Colombo Ma and Pa, as we have been able to forgive the past and focus on just being a family. Ma Colombo is very supportive of the work I want to do for the Lord. Before they passed, I reconciled with my mother and father.

When I was new to the Christian lifestyle, I guess I expected a halo to be over my head that showed people that I was holy. Far from it. But I am still a work in progress. Both my parents and I have changed for the better. The Lord is the healer in all ways!

I have bought my first home, which was a big step for me. I have retired from cosmetology and am enjoying time with my family, doing volunteer work, and traveling. I talk to God all day every day—when I find a good parking spot, I say a quick prayer to thank God. I see Him in every part of my life. Every day, He shows me something different.

Here is a scripture that I always turn to. It means so much to me. It is Isaiah 40:1-2.

Comfort, yes, comfort my people, says your God. Speak comfort to Jerusalem, and cry out to her, that her warfare has ended, that her iniquity is pardoned, for she has received from the Lord's hand, double for all her sins.

I've shed many comforting tears by reading these verses.

Never, ever, do I want to be in any way self-righteous or forget what God has brought me through. I want to always remember that there are others like myself that still need deliverance and healing. I want to maintain the humility of Christ and keep my love and compassion for others, just as God has compassion on the widows and orphans. My desire is to always live by this scripture in Luke 10:27.

Love the Lord your God with all your heart and all your soul, and with all your strength and with all your mind. And love your neighbor as yourself.

In closing, I want to say that even the writing of this book has been very therapeutic, and I've enjoyed my closeness with God. I will pray for God's presence, protection, and provision for you. I pray that this book has touched your life in a powerful way for His glory!

GOD'S LOVE AND PLAN

God's holiness makes it impossible for Him to relate to sinful humanity, and His justice demands that the sinner be judged and condemned to eternal separation from God. Although God has every right to condemn man, because of His love, He provided a solution through His son, Jesus Christ, who bore the sins of man on the cross. Jesus' death was the only acceptable sacrifice for sin.

Nor is there salvation in any other, for there is no other name under heaven given among men by which we must be saved.

Acts 4:12

When Jesus died on the cross, He received the punishment we deserved. He was buried in a tomb, but He did not remain there. He resurrected. For all those who believe from the heart in His death, burial, and resurrection, you can have the guarantee of eternal life in the presence of God.

In God's mercy, He has given us free salvation through the death of His son, Jesus. You need to do five things to receive His precious salvation.

1. Acknowledge the problem of separation from God by your sin.
2. Admit to being a sinner and that you need salvation.
3. Recognize that Jesus died on the cross for your sins.
4. Commit your life to Jesus Christ, so that He can save you and guide you.
5. Receive Jesus Christ as your personal savior and Lord.

In Romans 10:9, the Bible says that *if you confess with your mouth, the Lord Jesus, and believe in your heart that God raised Him from the dead, you will be saved.*

A PRAYER TO RECEIVE JESUS CHRIST

Lord Jesus, I know that I am a sinner and am separated from God. Therefore, I ask You to forgive me of my sins. I believe You died for me and You paid the debt for my sins. I turn away from my sins and give my life to You, to live as You want me to live. I ask You now to come into my life and be my personal savior. Help me now to follow You and obey You as Lord. Allow me to discover Your good and perfect will for my life.

YOU HAVE RECEIVED ETERNAL LIFE

When you prayed to receive Jesus Christ as Savior and Lord of your life, He heard you, and several things took place. Your sins were forgiven, you became a child of God, and you received eternal life. Based upon God's word, this has happened to you, no matter how you feel.

Now, on a daily basis, talk to God in prayer, read His word, the Bible, every day, and fellowship with other Christians for support and spiritual guidance. Get into a good Bible-believing, Christ-following church. Welcome to the big family of God!

Robin Colombo, the widow of a boss of the big Ma Colombo family, tells how God brought her out of years of wandering in the wilderness of life. From a child, she experienced a deep broken heart and pursued the vain search for true love in her teens and twenties. Later, as a mafia wife, she fought the mob, the feds, endured physical and mental abuse, practiced witchcraft, attempted suicide twice, and was addicted to alcohol and drugs. She also survived several prison terms while trying to maintain her sanity. In her early forties, she was left with nothing and barely living. At forty-three, however, she found the true meaning of love and life through Jesus Christ. This true story will grip your heart like no other book.